Mindfulness and Meditation

Simple Mindfulness Techniques and Yoga Postures to Relieve Stress

(Remove Worry and Depression While Living With Peace and Happiness)

James Wilkins

Published by Rob Miles

© **James Wilkins**

All Rights Reserved

Mindfulness and Meditation: Simple Mindfulness Techniques and Yoga Postures to Relieve Stress (Remove Worry and Depression While Living With Peace and Happiness)

ISBN 978-1-989990-90-2

All rights reserved. No part of this guide may be reproduced in any form without permission in writing from the publisher except in the case of brief quotations embodied in critical articles or reviews.

LEGAL & DISCLAIMER

The information contained in this book is not designed to replace or take the place of any form of medicine or professional medical advice. The information in this book has been provided for educational and entertainment purposes only.

The information contained in this book has been compiled from sources deemed reliable, and it is accurate to the best of the Author's knowledge; however, the Author cannot guarantee its accuracy and validity and cannot be held liable for any errors or omissions. Changes are periodically made to this book. You must consult your doctor or get professional medical advice before using any of the suggested remedies, techniques, or information in this book.

Upon using the information contained in this book, you agree to hold harmless the Author from and against any damages, costs, and expenses, including any legal fees potentially resulting from the application of any of the information provided by this guide. This disclaimer applies to any damages or injury caused by the use and application, whether directly or indirectly, of any advice or information presented, whether for breach of contract, tort, negligence, personal injury, criminal intent, or under any other cause of action.

You agree to accept all risks of using the information presented inside this book. You need to consult a professional medical practitioner in order to ensure you are both able and healthy enough to participate in this program.

Table of Contents

INTRODUCTION 1

CHAPTER 1: WHAT IS MINDFULNESS? 9

CHAPTER 2: BASIC MINDFULNESS MEDITATION TECHNIQUE OR VIPASSANA MEDITATION 27

CHAPTER 3: WHAT IS MINDFULNESS 30

CHAPTER 4: HOW TO BENEFIT FROM THIS BOOK 37

CHAPTER 5: WHY ACCEPTANCE AND ACTION ARE VITAL? 43

CHAPTER 6: WHAT IS MINDFULNESS? 58

CHAPTER 7: MINDFULNESS... 61

CHAPTER 8 : THE PURPOSE OF MINDFULNESS 67

CHAPTER 9: HOW TO EAT MINDFULLY............................. 74

CHAPTER 10: THE BASIS OF MINDFULNESS...................... 77

CHAPTER 11: STRESS 89

CHAPTER 12: THE CONCEPT OF DELIBERATE THINKING . 101

CHAPTER 13: THE VALUE OF MINDFULNESS 105

CHAPTER 14: MINDFULNESS MEDITATION 112

CHAPTER 15: PRACTICING MINDFULNESS...................... 118

CHAPTER 16: WHAT IS MINDFULNESS? 125

CHAPTER 17: WHAT IS MINDFULNESS? 131

CHAPTER 18: WHAT IS MINDFULNESS? 136

- **CHAPTER 19: WELCOME** 141
- **CHAPTER 20: HOW TO PRACTICE MINDFULNESS** 151
- **CHAPTER 21: WHY YOU SHOULD CONSIDER VISUALIZING** 156
- **CHAPTER 22: A SIMPLE EXPLANATION OF MINDFULNESS** 161
- **CHAPTER 23: WHAT MINDFULNESS IS AND HOW TO PRACTICE IT** 167
- **CHAPTER 24: MINDFULNESS UNRAVELED** 171
- **CONCLUSION** 180

Introduction

Mindfulness is technically a state of mind enabling you to be constantly aware of your thoughts and actions. Mindfulness is also the term used to describe techniques used to keep your brain focused on the present. Mastering these mindfulness techniques will enable you to center yourself, develop a deeper understanding of yourself, and manage or minimize negativity in your life. The positive benefits of mindfulness on your overall health are measurable, and include increased emotional control and stability, improving overall physical health, mental outlook, inspiration and spiritual connection.

Do I need mindfulness in my life?

Most people skate through life without examining their actions or purpose in life, either so concentrated on daily meaningless tasks and worries, or imprisoned by mistakes and failures from their past. By understanding and implementing mindfulness, you can train yourself to live in the present. Mindfulness is centered on living in the here and now, truly existing in the present, not weighted down by the past, nor filled with anxiety about the future. Researchers believe one of the key elements of happiness is the ability to focus on the moment at hand, and to be grateful for the simple things in life. Incorporating mindfulness into your life will train your mind to exist every day with heightened awareness of your current reality, releasing the stress and anxiety, negative thoughts and baggage of past events, and freeing you to enjoy your life, experiencing true happiness and serenity.

Examine the power of mindfulness.

As you continue to read, you will discover many benefits of mastering the techniques of mindfulness. As you become more skilled at practicing mindfulness techniques, you will find you are able to greatly reduce your stress and anxiety, resulting in a more relaxed state, optimistic attitude, and overall feeling of confidence and well-being. The ability to focus on the present and remain calm has exponential effects, including enjoying the world around you, easier problem-solving, and a reduction of stress-induced physical problems. Mindfulness can contribute to optimum immune system function, better sleeping habits, and increased joy. The time and effort to implement mindfulness techniques is relatively small, yet the benefits are noticeable and numerous.

Where do I begin on the path to mindfulness?

Breathing is the mindfulness technique most commonly learned first. Mastering breathing is a powerful mindfulness asset which enables you to quickly calm and focus yourself. You can use the breathing technique anytime, anywhere, and it is immediately effective. This technique is also a fundamental part of all other mindfulness techniques, and is fairly easy to master.

To practice mindfulness of breathing, you need to start by sitting down somewhere where you won't be distracted. Next, make sure that you are comfortable and close your eyes. It is usually best if the room is dark. Your breathing is going to be your object of concentration, so start by breathing in through your nose slowly.

Be aware of the sensation of inhaling and how it makes you feel. Nothing else enters your mind. Feel your chest expand. Now slowly exhale through your mouth, again experiencing every sensation. If this technique is difficult for you, don't worry. With practice, mindfulness breathing will become second nature.

Remain focused on your breath and how it touches your nose, your chest, and your mouth. You can use a counting system to know how much time to spend on your mindfulness session. On each exhale, count from one to ten, and then in reverse order. When you arrive at one, you've taken your final exhale for the mindfulness session. Take a minute to be aware of how you feel. Your body should now be relaxed, and your mind should be clear.

Exactly what are the benefits of mindfulness to my overall health and wellness?

The benefits of mindfulness are numerous. One of the most important and far-reaching benefits is stress reduction. Everyone experiences a certain level of stress, but if your mind is continually filled with debilitating thoughts, anxiety, and worry, the effects on your body and mind are negative and cumulative. Mastering mindfulness techniques will enable you to focus your mind on your present life and surroundings, releasing negative stress, anger, worry, and tension, and allowing your mind and body to exist in an increased, calmer state of awareness. Achieving mindfulness will have a positive effect on your mind and your body.

To achieve results, practice at least one mindfulness technique every day. It is important to be consistent. If you wish, you may implement more than one technique at a time to feel faster results, or to focus on a particular issue you are trying to improve.

Is mindfulness as simple as it seems?

The concept of mindfulness is simple, and some of the techniques are very easy to learn. However, the habits and thoughts which prevent you from keeping your mind in the present are often complex and have built up over years, so it takes time to develop new patterns and habits. It takes discipline to focus your mind, and mindfulness breathing is the first step of many toward achieving mindfulness. Learning and consistently practicing the mindfulness techniques will enable you to successfully understand how to achieve mindfulness, and the more you concentrate and practice, the easier achieving mindfulness will become.

Will I see immediate improvement when I incorporate mindfulness into my life?

The answer is yes and no. You will probably find you immediately feel more relaxed and focused just by implementing the mindfulness breathing techniques. By trying to be more mindful, you may become more aware of your present surroundings, and you will begin to realize just how much you allowed your mind to be filled with negative or counterproductive thoughts. It takes time and perseverance to fully implement all of the mindfulness techniques, but you will see a number of benefits and improvements if you consistently learn and use the techniques. Over time, you will learn to remain in the present, releasing the weight of past worries, and refusing to burden your thoughts with future anxieties. Mindfulness techniques will positively impact you immediately, but the greatest benefits will be realized over time as you strive to become a more positive and calm person.

If you are practicing mindfulness throughout the day, at least once daily, you're more likely to notice results quickly. You are also more likely to notice a shift in your overall mental state and energy levels. Of course, if you're using more than one of these techniques, you're also going to notice a more significant change because you're targeting your entire lifestyle instead of just small areas of it.

Chapter 1: What Is Mindfulness?

Before jumping into dissecting how mindfulness can help you, it is important to take a step back and actually understand what mindfulness is. I mean, you've probably heard of it a lot, but do you actually know what it is? If you don't know what it is, how can you expect to know you've attained it?

A more interesting question to ponder over is whether mindfulness is something that can even be attained. In Western culture, we've structured our lives around the chasing of goals and objectives. A life without a goal is a pointless existence, so we've been told. Everyone needs to have a defined ambition and things aren't given to you, you have to go out and grab them.

This is true of material things and the stuff you don't have but how can you grab at something you already have? This is the conundrum about mindfulness; most people in our society fail to understand.

You see, you already have the ability to be mindful. You just need to allow it.

Brain Surgery

Mindfulness as a practice finds its origins in ancient Buddhist principles but its versatility is such that it has been adopted by a wide variety of religions since. Indeed, all of the major religions of this world have sections devoted to being mindful and being present in every task that we do.

Presence is what is central to mindfulness. By being present you're acknowledging the only instant in time you have available to you. However, mindfulness goes beyond just being present. The true crux of the practice is observation. Adopting a third person's viewpoint of your thoughts and actions is what all mindfulness boils down to.

So, if you think about it, what you're doing is analyzing your own brain. This is why mindfulness is so difficult to practice. It's easy to think that you can be present and focus completely on what you're doing right now but reality offers a different experience. Try focusing on your breath this instant. Notice how you inhale and exhale and try to explore the quality of your breath.

Notice whether it's hot or cold. Where does it hit your skin on exhalation? Can you feel where it goes when you inhale? Now, think back to what your mind was doing as you were observing your breath. Odds are that it was focused on something else or that it was bringing up weird images in your mind.

Then there are those people who claim to be fully focused. There are only two groups of people who experience this state. The first are the truly enlightened and they are unlikely to be reading this book. The second are the rank beginners. This is because such people are not even aware of what their mind is doing.

I'm not mentioning this to make you feel bad. It's just a fact. The good news is that you're going to learn exactly how much of a chatterbox your mind can be and why ignoring it for the most part is one of the best things you'll do in your life.

Greater Understanding

Buddhist philosophy views mindfulness as being the path one needs to take in order to understand the truth about the universe. There's a lot of moving parts to that statement, so let's break it down a bit. First is the detail regarding mindfulness being a path. You see, practicing mindfulness isn't just about doing a few exercises, as I've mentioned before, it's about living a certain way.

As you live mindfully, you'll learn more about yourself and how your mind reacts. When you keep progressing along this path, at some point, you'll realize that you can observe the same delusions you operate under in others around you. You'll begin to detect that point in time where your brain or the other person's brain chooses to react to the sensory stimulus they receive.

You'll notice that between the moment when something happens to you and the moment when you decide to react to it, there exists a gap. The gap is the most peaceful state of being and true presence is found here. It will be a fleeting thing and you will chase it. Once you chase it enough, you'll realize that it has always been there, and you need to allow it to exist instead of running after an image of it.

This is just a small taste of the path that will unfold before you. Everyone experiences things differently and this is why mindfulness isn't a path of understanding the world as much as it is all about figuring out who you are. Is there even a difference between understanding yourself and the universe? You'll find out!

This brings us to the next portion of our initial sentence which talks about "understanding." What is understanding and what is knowledge? Often the two are confused for one another. Who is better equipped to deal with the world, a person who has excellent interpersonal skills or a recluse genius mathematician? Obviously, it's the former. But who's understands things better?

Who has a better grasp of reality? This opens another line of thought. What is reality? The journey you will undertake will bring about all sorts of questions like these. It is easy and very pleasing to our ego to sit around and pontificate about all of these things, but the fact is that all of our opinions about these things are worth as much as piece of garbage in the overall scheme of things.

Doing and practicing is what counts when it comes to mindfulness and without practice, you cannot hope to acquire any knowledge. The true nature of knowledge is thus the journey itself and not the destination. Along the way, as you observe what triggers you, you'll gain a deeper insight into what the nature of your reality is and how you have created it.

Reality is created by your intention. Intention is a nebulous thing and cannot be described with any great accuracy. Intention can be best thought of as the spirit with which you live your life. Ancient Buddhism opines that by fixing the right intention, a person's journey in life becomes that much easier. What is the right intention? Briefly, it is to practice right action and right thought.

What is right action and thought? Well, at this point we'd be going deep into Buddhist philosophy and that is not the point of this book. The aim is to apply mindfulness to achieve improvements in your life, namely by reducing the amount of stress you experience. So, let's just say that your actions and intentions need to be aligned on achieving a more harmonious view with the world.

This means you need to align yourself with the reality that is around you. The more your reality conflicts with what is around you, universal reality so to speak, the greater the stress and disconnect you will experience. You expect things to go left but the world goes right. You undertake stress.

You think you're qualified for the job, but your boss doesn't and promotes someone else instead. Stress. The world is loaded with all kinds of stress triggers for us and the mistake we make is that we try to change the world. If a loved one behaves a certain way, that annoys us, what is our typical reaction? Well, if you're like most people, you probably tell them to cut it out. You try to get them to stop.

Mindfulness will get you to realize that you cannot control things which are outside of you. The more you try to control them, the more out of sync with reality you become and the more the suffering you heap on yourself. In this context, suffering can be thought of as being stressed.

Think back to what happens when you keep telling your loved one to change their behavior. One day they simply refuse, and this results in a dramatic fight. Good luck not getting stressed out from that! True wisdom recognizes that change only comes from within since this is the only aspect of your life you fully control. Everything else is out of your hands and you have no business worrying about or trying to control any of that.

Progression

So, your intention is fixed to trying to align yourself to the world and to reduce the disconnect between inside and outside. What happens now? Well, once your intention changes you begin expressing this with your thoughts and words. These are what create your reality and are how people form impressions of you.

Really what's happening is that your intention is what creates your environment. The environment we surround ourselves with is extremely important. Research has shown that we mimic the actions and behavior of the people closest to us (ANTONOPOULOS,

2016). Everything from money, success and behavior is molded by your environment, whether when you were a child or an adult.

A lot of people try to change the outside world, again, by trying to force their worldview on their environment, that is, the people around them. Some even succeed for a while but this is the wrong way to go about things. Trying to control the thoughts and the will of others is a futile task and when it does blow up, it's pretty spectacular. Think back to how any dictator or despot has received their comeuppance.

Here, again, we see that the thing to do is to change your intention and allow this to change your environment. The actions you need to take are very little in this case. After all, you only need to seek to align yourself with where you want to be in your life. One of the biggest causes of stress is the fact that people are in one place and they want to be in another.

They might say their intention is to be elsewhere, but intention is betrayed by action. If a person continues to behave in the old manner or doesn't seem to be making any effort with regards to changing their situation, you can safely assume their intention is exactly where they are right now.

What you think and say is what creates actions and how you act is how you'll behave. Your behavior is the sum of everything you want and currently believe. There is usually a disconnect when it comes to our beliefs and our intention. This isn't as big of a deal as it sounds. I mean to say that if you're in one place and want to get to another, it is obvious you're going to have to learn new things to get there.

Your belief system is shaped by your environment and thus, if you set your intention right, the environment you need will be created by you and this will have an effect on your beliefs. Your beliefs in turn will further shape your environment and thus the feedback loop goes on and on.

It is in your interest to create a virtuous feedback loop instead of a vicious one as you can imagine. Your behavior will eventually come to define who you are in the eyes of the world. The sum of your behavior in various situations is what is called character. Character is what draws people and positive situations into your life and is what people ultimately see when they look at one another.

It is easy to adopt someone's character when looking to model a successful outcome, but the fact is that you need to dig deeper and figure out what their intention is. Intention is what guides everything and is the root of your existence. Fix your intention to be mindful and present and you'll create an environment which supports this, bit by bit.

Thought Patterns

Mindfulness will illuminate your thought patterns, as I've mentioned. By observing your mind, you'll be assuming the role of the impartial observer, not judging or questioning anything, but just observing. It sounds easy to do but the reality is a lot different. After all, you're the one you're observing, and it is hard to do this without making things personal.

If you're careening towards disaster, should you remain impersonal? No one can. The issue is that almost everything can seem like a disaster and the process of figuring out what is a big deal and what isn't is a lot like having a bandage ripped off on an unhealed wound. It hurts.

Mindfulness isn't a passive process. It requires you to sit there and take stock of things and remain steadfast on your path. If anything, it is the most active process out there because this is how you engage in life and create a reality for yourself. There are two ways of practicing mindfulness, formal and informal.

The formal method is what monks do, which is to say that they dedicate their lives to the practice and spend long stretches of the day in meditation. Every action of theirs is informed by spiritual prescription. The informal method is to bring mindfulness to everyday actions. For example, if you're eating, becoming mindful of what you're eating and of being fully present without distraction is practicing informal mindfulness.

Personally, I find a mixture of both is the best way forward. This establishes a mindset of continuous practice and improvement. Set aside some time every day to conduct a formal practice but also keep practicing as you go about your day to the best of your abilities. Remember, if you set your intention to be mindful, you will create an environment which will encourage you to practice mindfulness.

Let's look at an example of mindful practice. Since I've mentioned eating something, we might as well begin with this. Let's say you're eating almonds and want to be more mindful of it. Pick up a single almond and begin:

The aim is to explore the almond with all of your senses. This is what it means to be aware of something. Set your intention as such. Act as if you've never seen it before (and you probably never truly have).

Run your fingers over the ridges and feel how coarse it is. Does the coarseness vary depending on the region of the almond? How do the edges feel? Do they pierce your fingers?

What is the shape of the solitary nut like? Keep running your fingers to understand it and feel the texture. It feels rough for sure. What about the temperature of the skin? Is it hot, cold, room temperature? As you press onto the almond can you feel your pulse in your fingertips?

How does it feel in the palm of your hand? It feels small, doesn't it? Roll it around a little between your fingers and notice how different fingers react to it. As you switch fingers can you feel the new sense of touch running from your fingers to the inside your body via your nerves?

Now, smell it. Does it have a smell at all? What does it remind you of, if it does?

Think about wanting to eat the almond. Notice how the minute you think about it, your arm automatically moves and brings it closer to your mouth. Now, open your mouth and place it on your tongue without chewing it.

Roll it around inside and notice how your mouth becomes wet with saliva. This happens automatically and you didn't have to do anything to generate it. You didn't even think about it. Notice how your body is like a machine that just does things on autopilot.

As you're rolling it inside your mouth, think back to the thoughts that have been running through your head since the first step. What have they been? What words have they contained? Notice your reactions to those words. Don't judge, just notice and let them go. Once this is done, get back to your almond.

Bite it and begin to chew it. The texture feels a lot different. Notice the sound that is generated when you chew. What does your tongue feel like when the almond's insides hits your taste buds?

Swallow the almond and feel it pass down your throat. Notice any other internal sensations as this happens.

This exercise is just a taste of what mindfulness is all about. I'd like to note that you don't need to consciously think in this manner each and every time you do these things. Once you set your intention to be mindful, your body will follow, and you will begin to notice these things all by yourself.

As you do this, notice the number of things that are going on within you and around you. Do you realize how much of your world you simply take for granted? Think of all the things happening within your body right now. That solitary almond is contributing to this machine that is in your possession. How cool is that!

You see, this is what mindfulness does. It awakens you to things you cannot see with your eyes. Now that you've got a taste of mindfulness, let's move forward and establish a base for your mindfulness practice.

Chapter 2: Basic Mindfulness Meditation Technique Or Vipassana Meditation

People from Western countries usually use this most basic meditation technique. This technique helps relieve stress. It also promotes self-acceptance and it improves your cognitive function. This practice is also perfect for beginners as it is quite simple and easy to do.

Before you begin this practice, it's important that you wear comfortable clothes. Also, do this in a place or a room where you will not be disturbed. Turn off your mobile phone and all other distractions. You can also light some incense sticks or scented candles to enhance your experience. It can also help if you do some stretching exercises or do some yoga poses before starting. This will condition your body so it will be easier for you to focus. It's also important to set an alarm. This allows you to focus on your practice without having to check the clock. Remember that it takes a while to reap the benefits of mindfulness meditation so it's important that you're committed to it. You have to set aside a couple of minutes every day for your mindfulness meditation practice.

Sit in a comfortable position. You can sit on a chair or you can sit on the floor in a cross-legged position. Do not lie down as you may fall asleep during the process.

Close your eyes and take deep breaths. Inhale through your nose and exhale through your mouth.

As you breathe in, say silently "inhaling". As you breathe out, say silently "exhaling".

Try to focus only on your breath.

It is likely that you will get some distracting thoughts, especially when you have an untrained mind. You may think about something trivial like food or movies. When this happens, simply acknowledge these thoughts and then bring your focus back to your breath. You may have to do this many times, especially during your first few sessions.

Once you hear the alarm. Say a silent prayer of gratitude and open your eyes.

This technique is one of the exercises used in Dr. Kabat-Zinn's MBSR or Mindfulness-Based Stressed Reduction program. This technique helps relax your body and it also strengthens your mind.

You can do this in your bedroom or in the office. You can do this technique any time of the day, but when you're still jumpstarting your meditation practice, it is important to do this in the morning as your mind is still fresh and a lot easier to control. You can do this for about 3-5 minutes during your first week and you can increase your mindfulness meditation practice by a few minutes as you progress. Most Zen masters do this for more than 3 hours a day!

Chapter 3: What Is Mindfulness

In mindfulness you are learning to pay attention, on purpose, in the present moment, without judgement.

Mindfulness has got a lot to do with the "Beginner's Mind", just like the mind of a child that discovers new things. So whatever your situation or experience is, the idea is to be curious about what is happening within yourself.

Mindfulness can be used every moment in your life. You can use it to take better care of yourself, work with mental barriers, learn to be present instead of living in autopilot, recognize patterns of reactivity, cope with stress, and learn to respond instead of react.

Mindfulness can be practiced anytime, anywhere. When you are still, when you are moving, when you are eating, when you are calm or under stress.

All of these aspects will be approached in this book and you will start with an exercise that you can do when you have the chance to sit and eat without rush. Ideally once a day. This is called the "Raisin Exercise".

Exercise – Raisin Exercise

Get a raisin and look at it with a beginner's mind. Look as if you've never seen it before. Whatever it is that you eat, show interest in it, appreciate it, and don't just eat automatically. Use your senses! Take your time doing this exercise.

First of all, see it. Look at the raisin.

What colors does it have? Is it just one color or a mixture of colors?

What shape does it have?

What is your mind doing while you look at it? Any memories or associations? Or maybe thinking about something else?

Feel it with the fingertips.

What texture does it have?

How does it feel in your skin?

Bring it to the ear, press and roll the raisin with the fingers.

What are you thinking and hearing as this is happening?

Does it remind you about something?

Bring it to the nose and smell it.

Smell it with one nostril at a time, if possible. Do you feel any differences?

Close your eyes. How does your sensing change?

Any thoughts, feelings, or memories?

Feel it with the lips. Don't bite it. Just feel it with the lips.

Feel its texture, temperature, and maybe the first flavor.

Let it go inside the mouth but don't bite it yet. Just actually taste it.

Again realize the texture, the flavor, the temperature inside the mouth.

Bite and chew.

Notice what's going on in your mouth as you chew.

Raisin Exercise Summary

Sight – Observe the colors and shape.

Touch – Feel the texture.

Hearing – Acknowledge the sounds.

Smell – Sense the scent.

Taste – First feel it with the lips. Then bite and chew. Feel the aroma, texture, temperature and the sensations inside the mouth.

Tips to Remember!

- You can do this exercise the same way with any food or meal that you like. Just follow these quick guidelines.

- At any time you can close your eyes to realize the difference in your senses.

- Acknowledge when you become distracted by the thoughts and come back to the senses.

- It is very important not to rush. Take your time and enjoy the food.

 Self-Reflection

What's in your mind after this exercise?

Why do you think you are doing this?

Sensing vs Thinking

This is for you to think about. The mind or the brain cannot do two things at once. It cannot do sensing and thinking at the same time. This is a neuroscience fact.

The mind can be in a thinking mode or it can be in a sensing mode. When it's sensing it's not thinking, because when the mind is sensing it interrupts the processing. It interrupts the thoughts.

When one is working the other one is not working, so you can interrupt thinking or processing when you sense.

Let me give you an example. If you stroke a cat, you can't be thinking about anger, sadness, or anything else. If you are stroking a cat's back and can really feel the warmth and softness of the fur, you cannot be thinking about something else. You might go very quickly between the thoughts and the warmth of the fur, but when you sense you interrupt the processing.

It can give you relief from overthinking. When you are stressed or anxious or depressed because you overthink, if you are sensing - and you can sense with the mind, not just with the other senses - you can't be thinking. This is very important. You can come to your senses to relax from difficulties, relieve from overthinking, and let the mind rest.

This is a very important exercise that you can do every day, not just with food but with any other daily activities, like brushing the teeth, taking a shower, walking in the park, or any other activity you like. Everyday pick an activity, especially one that gives you pleasure and use the senses to relieve your mind from overthinking. When you finish reading this book you will find a Pleasurable Activities List to help you on this daily exercise.

Chapter 4: How To Benefit From This Book

So, you've probably read the previous chapter and you're beginning to wonder about how to begin your meditation journey. It is a good question.

You start this journey just like any other one you may embark on. You start with the first step. The first step is to recognize and embrace the idea that you do not know anything about meditation. In other words, you start at the beginning, with an open mind.

An open mind allows you to take in the information in a nonbiased way. Some of the ideas regarding meditation may seem farfetched and unrealistic to you, but if you look at them that way, you will never get the full benefits available to you.

The analogy of learning is like an onion has been used in works before. Basically, learning starts with a very basic principle and as you learn more, another layer is added. As you learn more, another layer and another is added until you learn what you need to know.

Don't become impatient with the process. If you do, you will defeat the total objective of learning meditation. Also, keep in mind there is no time limit on how fast, or slow, you learn and employ the principles in this work. Meditation is always a work in progress, and you will set yourself up for defeat if you do not keep an open mind.

A few tips to help you plan for success:

Designate a certain time of day and place to meditate. I know, this may not be possible every single day, but by first setting the intention of it, it will help you to get into the mindset, help eliminate distractions, and help you work it into your day

While most meditations require very little equipment (perhaps a mat or chair), there are some meditations which require you to move about or walk. There is also a meditation we will discuss which will require you to lay down, so find enough room to allow for that.

Keep in mind that there are several different meditations included in this work. Not all of them may work for you or may not be feasible depending on your health status. Say, for instance, walking is difficult for you, then you may not be able to do the walking form of meditation described.

Keep in mind too that anything that contributes positively to your life or wellness is worth exploring and using. Keeping an open mind will help you explore these practices and hopefully find the perfect one for you.

Research has shown that meditation can work in as little as four days. Forming it as a habit can take up to a couple of months.

Keep a meditation journal. By keeping a small inexpensive notebook with you, you will be able to track your progress. Write down your thoughts about the exercise, if you had trouble with it, what you experienced. It may help to look back later to see which technique works best for you.

We will start with the simplest types of meditation. Remember the onion analogy? So, the simplest forms of meditation will come first, and more difficult will follow. We strongly suggest you do not skip ahead, but take each meditation in turn, trying it before moving on to the next.

Skipping a day or exercise, while not it will halt your progress, it's not worth freaking out over either. However, to learn these practices in the proper order, just pick up where you left off, not skipping the daily exercise you missed to stay on track.

Having said that, if you want to read the book from beginning to end before actually starting the list, feel free to do so. Some folks want to know ahead of time what they are letting themselves in for.

That's fine too. This is about your life. Your meditation. You are in control.

At the end of each chapter, you will find suggestions and questions. You'll also find a suggestion on how to go deeper into each meditation technique if you choose too.

This may seem like a lot of information, and it is. But you also need to keep in mind that all types of meditation, no matter what style or cultural affiliation it has, teaches the same skill set:

Concentration

Focus

Awareness

Self-regulation

If you get bored with one type of practice, there are plenty more. Sitting is the most employed strategy since sitting still can help you calm your thoughts and mind. If, however, you are one of those people who find it physically impossible to sit still I am one of those people myself-perhaps walking is the meditation that you want to use.

Through this work, you will find words and phrases that you may be unfamiliar with. These words will be in italics and will also be found in the glossary at the back of this work. So, if you run into one of these, please check out the dictionary so that it will be clearer for you.

Another thing to remember is that not everyone likes every style of meditation. If you come across one that you start and find that you either don't like it or are physically unable to complete it, stop and repeat the previous day's exercise. Be sure to make a note in your journal as to what happened, why, and how you coped with the exercise.

Questions:

What four skills sets are needed to practice meditation? Do you feel you are lacking any of them?

What are you going to do to increase those skill sets you feel you are lacking in?

A goal without a plan is just an intention. What are you going to do to make meditation a regular part of your life? What are your action steps?

Chapter 5: Why Acceptance And Action Are Vital?

Like many people, you may gauge whether you are successful or perhaps not by how you invest your time, not by that which you believe or even just how you think about it. This's another way of thinking that the actions of yours in daily life, no matter how big or perhaps small, bring up to what your living is approximately. It is just with the actions of yours, what you should do to move the life of yours in the instructions you would like it to go.

When you behave in ways contrary to the aspirations of yours, you get psychologically and emotionally stuck. This is exactly why we will not provide some quick or cheap fixes like the people you hear each day from the media and the culture of ours in general. You understand the message: eliminate your suffering and pain, after which you will be pleased and also have the life you need.

Becoming a pain free is actually no promise of an important life. A good number of people appear to have no discomfort and barely any worries and nevertheless they are unsatisfied with the way of life they lead. We also know a large number of people live with overwhelming pain as well as hardship and still organize to find dignity and meaning in the lives of theirs. They go about living every day as their last. You are able to do it as well. When you live every day as your last, things which seem extremely important suddenly appear less valuable, couple of exercises builds on this notion within the chapters to come.

Learning to view the thoughts of yours with mild, dispassionate interest and no entanglement will even enable you to discover how you can quit letting anxiety keep on to be a monster that seems controlling the life of yours. It will place one to break loose from nervousness by creating room for it. As you do this, you will be no cost to place your energy and attention into living a lifetime that you care profoundly about. As that occurs, fear and anxiety will be only a part of your life, not the quite fabric of the being.

Accept with serenity everything you can't change, possess the courage to alter what you are able to and improve the wisdom to find out the difference. Nearly all people realize it's a lot easier to go along with the serenity creed compared to do what it claims. That is because many people just do not understand what they can and can't change. Lots of more do not understand how to recognize and deal with thoughts as well as feelings that hurt. Even then, few understand the way to utilize this profound statement to the daily lives of theirs. We will explain to you exactly how to place the serenity creed into motion.

When you read through this book and carry out the exercises, you will discover ways to create the crucial difference between what you are able to or not to change. When you perform the mindfulness and acceptance exercises, you will discover ways to make room for many of the experiences of yours; the good, negative and hideous ones. With compassion & acceptance, you will discover ways to refocus the precious time of yours and effort on doing what matters for you. This will likely lead you to a brand new path out of your fears, anxieties and worries of your life.

How to use this book?

You're going to learn how to get your mind and your own life out of anxiety. The consciousness exercises and anxiety strategies you will be using are evidence-based; they have been shown to do the job. Awareness is one of the most powerful and productive methods to replace stress with peace of mind, calm and joy while exercises based on psychotherapy techniques have years of studies that demonstrate their effectiveness in reducing the signs of stress.

The subjects covered within this book will lead you through both consciousness ability and anxiety-oriented exercises. Plans will vary on construction tools to your awareness skill set and on exercises that cover different types or aspects of stress. Both kinds of skills are interrelated and closely connected. Learning about your anxiety and performing targeted exercises can allow you to experience fewer symptoms that are causing you problems; anxiety and evasion. At precisely the identical time learning awareness skills will allow you to produce more of what you are doing to have inner peace, calm and also the ability to enjoy life. All exercises reinforce and encourage one another to supply you with a good base to grow.

Choose a new approach to get a different outcome

Your daily life is a sacred travel. It's all about discovery, change, growth, movement, transformation, continuously expanding your vision of what's possible, stretching your soul and figuring out how to determine clearly and deeply, listening to your intuition, shooting courageous challenges at every step along the way. You are on the path of just the place you're meant to be correct today and from here, you may only move forward, shaping your life story into a magnificent tale of triumph of healing, courage, beauty, awareness, energy, dignity and also of love.

This chapter is all about preparing the way for something fresh in your life. Just as we all hate to admit it, we understand that to receive a different result we have to alter what we're doing today. This is a great mantra we utilize in our personal lives. The mantra goes something like that:

"If I will continue to do what I've always done, then I'm likely to get exactly what I have always got."

Here's the great news: you can choose a fresh approach to find a different result in your life. This new strategy is what you will get within this workbook. You'll realize that the material in this publication can allow you to act in your nervousness and your life differently by placing you in charge of everything you can control. Quite simply, you are able to control and change how you respond to your anxiety-related feelings, thoughts, and worries:

You can stop trying to cope with anxieties and fears (if working along with other management approaches haven't worked in a lasting manner).

You can learn how to leave anxieties, worries and anxieties independently and simply experience them as thoughts, feelings or even painful memories.

You do not need to act in your own anxiety and it does not need to drive what you do. As much as you really feel like running from intense stress, you can learn how to act otherwise. You can learn to watch anxious feelings and painful thoughts and not to do exactly what they let you do.

You can learn how to move with your anxious discomfort and also do something that's potentially vital in your life.

We know from clinical and research expertise that the remedy to worry, nervousness and anxiety is not a battle. It's not about trying to attract them down when they rear their ugly heads. It's not about attempting to get rid of them. It's also not about combating or replacing negative with positive ideas. You know this conflict firsthand and so do we. You may believe that you must win it, may be by trying harder, fighting more, learning better approaches, reading about stress issues, finding a new medicine, venting and so on.

The truth is that: this conflict cannot be won. But here's more good news that you don't need to win this battle in order to start living the life you would love to contribute. As you use this publication, we'll demonstrate why this can be a rigged game where the solutions to everyday sources of pain from the world around you are being implemented in places where they don't really get the job done.

For today, we request that you amuse the chance that the answer to your anxiety issues is not to battle" better or harder". The remedy is to modify your relationship and your answer to your anxious thoughts and feelings. You can optimise to quit fighting. To get there, you'll need to understand to acknowledge nervous thoughts and feelings without getting mad & acting on them doing exactly what they say.

As we direct you in learning those skills, we will help you develop compassion for yourself and to your nervousness and other painful experiences. You will also rediscover what really matters for you: you'll concentrate on what you want your life to stand for and then behave in ways that move you ahead on your own life, even if this means attracting worries, anxieties and fears or other unwanted thoughts and feelings along for the journey.

This might not be the first book offering a new connection with anxiety. Nonetheless, it's the first book that'll teach you how you can cultivate that connection with compassion and acceptance with both eyes focused entirely on assisting you to live your daily life with purpose and meaning.

Our goal is to assist you to spend your precious time in this world doing what you care intensely about instead of spending your time and energy seeking to control stress. Keep this in mind while you work with the material in the publication. The prize we are after is that a life lived well, your lifestyle lived to its full!

What is ACT?

This workbook offers you away from your anxiety of your life. According to a revolutionary new strategy called acceptance and commitment therapy (ACT, pronounced as "act"). This pronunciation is critical because it summarizes what ACT ultimately stands for: committed ACTion.

Accept--Choose--Take Action

The easiest way to get the gist of ACT will be to concentrate on what the three letters stand for: Accept-- Pick --Take action. Put another way, ACT is all about letting go, showing up to a lifetime and end up moving in directions you would like to go. Don't worry if that strikes you as overly general or idealistic. We are going to get more specific as you possibly move on and practice the exercises.

For today, we'll change the ACT acronym just a bit to offer you a feeling of what is to come.

Accept

This is step one in ACT and also a step that we'll help you nurture over within this workbook and we expect during your lifetime. It entails active abilities that'll enable you to react differently; with kindness, compassion, gentleness, much less involvement as anxieties, fears and other sources of emotional and mental pain show up. The idea is to take what you are already having anyway. This ability disarms the struggle you're doing with undesirable thoughts and feelings. As you learn to let go, your distress will go too. With that, the need to eliminate or change those thoughts and emotions rips-off.

After you drop the rope on your tug-of-war with your anxiety monsters, you will notice your hands, toes, head and mouth is going to be freed up to put to use for the things in life you truly care about. In the procedure, your daily life will grow and develop in ways that might have seemed impossible until now. Acceptance will assist you in making anxiety a part of your life.

Choose

The second step is about picking management for your life. It entails identifying exactly what you value in life and what you want your life to stand for. It is about assisting you to discover what is really important to you; what you appreciate and then making a choice. What kind of child, sister or brother, student or friend do you want to be? What sorts of activities are meaningful to you? Answering these kinds of questions is about choice picking to go forward in directions that are uniquely yours and accepting what's inside you and that which includes you and accompanies you on the way. It is a step you will make time and time again.

Here your life is requesting you a significant question: Are you prepared to contact and remain in touch with your body and mind without avoiding or seeking to escape them? If the solution is no, you're getting bigger and your anxiety will grow larger. In case the solution is "yes", you'll get larger and your life will get bigger too. Living well will become your attention, not alive to feel and think well.

Take action

The next step entails taking actions toward realizing your valued life goals. It is about building a commitment to action and changing what you can change. This means learning how to behave in a way that moves you ahead in the path of your favorite values. As you use the content, you'll begin to find that there's a difference between you as an individual, your activities, thoughts and feelings that you have about yourself. You won't find us requesting you to just face your fears in the expectation of a better life. Our objective is to boost your willingness to maintain your internal psychological distress along with you at the service of your own life objectives and dreams.

You may feel intimidated by those 3 bold actions. In reality, you may be quite fearful. You will say: "That is too big, I can't do this". Should you feel this way or have other related notions and feelings that are alright. All we ask is that you just hold your ideas gently. Just keep the book in your hands. Take advantage of your eye to continue reading. Let the Ideas be exactly what they are and let them do what they're doing. Like other ideas and feelings, it is okay if they come, its okay if they stay and it is ok if they go.

Chapter 6: What Is Mindfulness?

With Mindfulness for Beginners, you can begin to learn about techniques through which you can change your relationship to the way you feel, think, work, and love -- and thus awaken to and demonstrate yourself more clearly. This book will teach you the necessary tools in which you can begin living a more free, happy and abundant life.

We continuously have our head occupied or full of thoughts about the past or future in our busy lives such as what are we going to become, what we are going to perform next or how well or badly we just performed. This means we are simply not aware of what exactly is around us regularly, and what is happening now.

It's a very simple kind of skill that anyone can get benefit from and learn from, and only a few minutes a day are required. Mindfulness involves being conscious of our current experience at any particular moment. Our present experience consists of our:

*What's our body trying to tell us? - Physical sensations

*What are we feeling? - Emotions

*What are we thinking? - Thoughts

*What do we hear, see, touch and feel? - Surrounding environment

To be mindful means - being completely aware of what is happening inside - our feelings and thoughts and what is around us, what we can hear, see, touch and feel. Mindfulness is all about learning how to observe all this but not worrying about it or getting caught up in thinking, so being able to, with a present and clear mind, decide what we then attend to.

Jon Kabat-Zinn, a well-known professional suggests that we may take a long time for our completeness, however, it's already ours and already here. Practicing mindfulness holds the chance of not just a short-lived sense of happiness, but a real acceptance of a deeper unity that shrouds and fills our lives.

Who doesn't want to live his/her life happily? We can do Mindfulness wherever we are and it is a key skill for happiness.

Mindfulness has been shown to help us be more relaxed, healthier, open to learning, happy, creative, and less affected by stress. It improves our sleep quality and relationships with people. Lastly, it helps us to be more satisfied with our lives.

Mindfulness is helpful all over the place, as it explores all parts of the body and mind. This type of meditation offers plenty of unseen benefits, such as building up skills to advance your life quality or being a helpful anchor to avoid the mind getting lost in feelings and thoughts. You may use this meditation to build up deeper concentration.

Chapter 7: Mindfulness

Mindfulness

Mindfulness meditation has become so popular in Denmark that more and more Danes take on mindfulness courses and mindfulness retreat at home and abroad.

Once you've read the detailed introduction to Mindfulness right here, we'd highly recommend you to visit our collective page about Mindfulness, which is constantly updated with the best selected blogs, events, talks with leading mindfulness teachers.

Here comes a detailed explanatory description and introduction into mindfulness and a guide.

There is a lot of writing about how mindfulness has its historical origin, where and how much mindfulness is being used today: in companies, in hospitals, in psychiatry, in psychology, in schools, and as (self) therapy form, etc. As a generally interested user It is therefore a little interesting to be informed about what mindfulness is so concrete and not least how to self-practice mindfulness meditation at home or somewhere else where you can be undisturbed for a while. Therefore, we have endeavored not only to explain what mindfulness is but also to give you a mindfulness guide that you can use right now and now.

What is Mindfulness?

In short, Mindfulness Meditation is a training of your mind where you exercise and strengthen being able to be present through full attention: on your thoughts, feelings and body sensations - as well as attention to your surroundings and relationships. You are therefore training to become more present and attentive present at every moment of your life. You train a self-perceiving "buffer" in your auto minds, actions, judgments over others, etc. You train to control the "auto pilot" of your mind - so you become more "Lord in your own house" - so you do not let yourself Make sure your thoughts just run around.

In order for you to feel a crucial difference when exercising mindfulness, it may definitely be advantageous for you to use guided mindfulness meditation daily, such as a guided mindfulness CD, podcast, itunes - especially if you are unable to go on A mindfulness team or course.

Mindfulness: What do you achieve by mindfulness training

With mindfulness, as you said, you are far better able to control your mind so that your mind and thoughts just do not control you. Mindfulness is just right to be present with full attention right here and right now, from moment to moment. It means having all the senses open and being aware of your thoughts, emotions and external senses. Without judging something, for example, it feels good or bad, etc. That means: without assessing what you are experiencing. Just register it as it is. And then let go of it without reacting to it.

In mindfulness you train the ultimate inner freedom: to escape the tyranny of mind and mind. This means that when we notice frustration or anger, we will be able to let it go faster without responding to it; That we can experience strong longing without being slave of it. This means that you do not let yourself throw away your spontaneous thoughts and feelings - what the Buddhists call "Monkey Mind" where your thoughts just jump and do and you follow. As you train Mindfulness, you will find yourself "distancing" from your thoughts and feelings - so you are no longer identical to your thoughts, experiences and feelings - but are relative to them. As humans, our mind has a mental "reaction space" between a thought or feeling and the time that goes before we respond or act on a thought or feeling. This "reaction space" can be small, as we see in people who are struggling to control pulses and therefore react immediately. Mindfulness meditation just expands your "reaction space" so you do not react or act (too) quickly or uncontrollably - which has many benefits in everyday life and in the intercourse with other people and for you to achieve more peace and soul To control stress symptoms.

With Mindfulness, you become a lot more lord in your own house, where you are able to consciously control your thoughts and feelings. How you want to relate to life, - to people you meet, situations you face, problems and challenges. As you consciously train your mind, you will be better able to choose how you want to experience what is happening in you and around you. How you choose to react to it.

When in a mindful state you have:

A funny mind

A better judgment

Control of your thoughts, reactions, and actions

And an acceptance of reality as it is

Mindfulness also gives you greater impulse control. That you manage to think about an extra time before you follow a desire for something inappropriate, for example to overeat, drink too much alcohol, etc.

In the following you will get insight into the different phases of a typical mindfulness mediation. The text is the basis of a Mindfulness CD that you can hear for free via myspace or buy and receive if you want a fully guided mindfulness training.

Chapter 8 : The Purpose Of Mindfulness

We all experience change constantly. Consistently. Change is the main consistent nowadays. It occurs and it happens quick. What are you doing pretty much the majority of the adjustment in your life? It is safe to say that you are opposing it? Giving it a chance to wash by you? Grasping it? Giving it a chance to take you where it will? I envision that a large portion of us do these things dependent on the change that is occurring at the time. Nonetheless, what might it resemble if we were more accountable for our reactions to change? What might it resemble if we were increasingly out before it?

We can be if we choose to lead a careful and purposeful life. By driving a careful and purposeful life I mean having an unmistakable mission, vision and set of qualities that guide our life and utilizing that to control by. When we utilize our own main goal, vision and qualities to manage us they act like a rudder giving us strength and helping us make course revisions as life gets extreme. They help us set our course when the going is smooth so as we see change seemingly within easy reach we have an approach to settle on choices about that change and can make sense of how to utilize it to further our potential benefit as opposed to consider it to be an immense hindrance.

Care and aim go past simply having an individual mission, vision and qualities. It is reflected by the way we approach our day by day living. It is reflected in the objectives we set for ourselves and by the way we approach achieving those objectives. Aim comes in with respect to how we address objective fulfillment. How are we going to approach accomplishing our objectives? How are we going to treat other individuals on route? What is our goal with each activity that we choose to take? What is our goal with our responses to things? Deliberate individuals have a genuine reason set out about how they are going to appear on the planet and how they will associate with the individuals in it.

At last care becomes possibly the most important factor. A careful individual is constantly mindful of himself and how he is collaborating with other individuals. He is completely mindful of how his activities sway others and of how they respond to him. He screens that and connects with his expectations to increase a beneficial outcome and result.

So you see goal and care have an inseparable tie to change - being responsible for the results of progress is a ground-breaking thing. Making sense of this isn't in every case simple. This may be an extraordinary time for you to get a mentor to help.

What is Mindfulness Meditation?

That involves focusing your mind in your experiences (such as your feelings, musings, and senses) right now.

Care manifestation can include breathing training, mental

Among the first institutionalized jobs for maintenance MBSR centers around consideration and mindfulness concerning the current. Other compact, frequent care hint mediations have been joined into medicinal settings to take care of stress, distress, a sleeping disease, along with other health ailments.

Instructor or application can help you when you begin (particularly in the event you're doing it for health purposes). A couple of people do it for 10 minutes, however a few minutes always can have any sort of effect. Here's a basic method for one to start:

1. Find a calm and pleasant place. Sit in a chair or on

2. Try to set apart all memories as time goes on and Stay at the current.

3. Be aware of your breath, focusing on the Belief of air moving throughout the human body as you relax. Feel your belly

rise and fall, and the atmosphere input your noses and depart from your mouth. Concentrate on the way each breath affects and is outstanding.

4. Watch every idea travel every which manner, no matter Whether it's a worry, fear, anxiety or anticipation. In the point when concerns appear on mind, do not dismiss or smother them nevertheless essentially note them keep quiet and use your breathing as a grapple.

5. Maybe You end up

6. Since the chance arrives to some local, sit for a Minute or two, becoming mindful of where you're. Get up gradually.

There is no law which says You Ought to sit on a pad at a Care intercession is 1 process, yet daily life provides a Whole Lot of opportunities to practice.3

Listed below are Kate Hanley's hints on creating care on your day by day program:

Have you ever at any stage found how nobody is The mix of time and bodily activity causes tidying to up after dinner an unbelievable time to try a small care.

Cleaning your teeth. You cannot go a day without cleaning Your teeth, which makes this daily job the perfect opportunity to deal with care. Feel your feet on the ground, the brush on your grip, your arm moving here and there. Einstein stated he did his very best justification while he was shaving- I would argue that what he was actually doing in these moments was rehearsing care!

Driving. It is anything but hard to daydream while You are driving, contemplating what to get for dinner or what you failed to perform at work daily. Use your drives of maintenance to maintain your thought moored to inside your car or truck.

Disposition killer the radio (or move it to something mitigating, very similar to older style), imagine your backbone creating tall, find the midpoint between loosening your hands up and holding the wheel also ardently, and take your own thought back into wherever you and your car are in distance at any stage you see your own mind meandering.

Working out. On the treadmill may make your workout to really go all the more quickly, however it will not do a whole lot to calm your mind. Make your health efforts a task in care by murdering all displays and focusing on your breathing and wherever your toes are in distance as you proceed.

Sleep time. Watch your struggles over sleep time together with the Kids vanish when you stop trying to rush through it and essentially Try to enjoy the experience. Cuddles you receive.

Chapter 9: How To Eat Mindfully

Eating mindfully is actually a great way to help determine how much you're eating and whether you're eating because you're hungry or just because you're bored. Use this exercise to eat mindfully. You can practice this exercise using a cracker, a raisin, a piece of chocolate, or a selection of crackers and fruit on a plate. Before you choose what you'll be eating, come to a place of mindfulness through sensing what your body needs. Notice what really makes you hungry when you look at it on the platter. Take your time and choose just one thing.

1. Now, focus with awareness of every movement it takes as you move your arm, hand, and fingers toward the piece of food and pick it up. Then focus on how you place it on your hand or hold it in your fingers.

2. Imagine that you've just found this new food and it's a new substance you've

never come across before. Explore this new food with your senses as if it were new. Take a close look at it, explore every bit of it with your eyes while it's sitting on your palm or in your fingers. Turn it around.

3. Notice the light and texture of it, the shape of the food, whether it's soft, coarse, hard, or smooth. Notice any thoughts that come about like 'why am I doing this?' Now see if you can just notice the thoughts and allow them to be before you bring your awareness back to the piece of food.

4. Take the piece of food and put it beneath your nose as you carefully notice the smell of it. Bring the piece of food to one of your ears, squeeze it, roll it around, and listen for any sound that comes from it. Begin to bring it back to your mouth and notice that the arm knows where to go. Notice how your mouth might be watering. Gently put it in your mouth or take a bite if it's larger than one bite-size. Do not chew yet! Feel it on your tongue,

the weight of it, size, temperature, and texture. Explore the sensations happening in your mouth.

5. When you're ready, intentionally bite down on the food. Does it go automatically to one side or stay on both sides? Notice when the flavor is released. Slowly chew and notice the changes in consistency as you chew it. When you're conscious of the impulse to swallow it, sense the food as it moves down your esophagus on its way to your stomach. Sit with that experience and notice any bits that might remain in the mouth, on the tongue, the taste, and feelings the food gives you.

6. Take a moment to be thankful for what you ate and practice with another piece or move on to just eating.

You can practice this exercise with just one piece of food or you can consume an entire plateful of food eating with mindfulness. If you're trying to lose weight, then try to practice this with every mouthful of food you take.

Chapter 10: The Basis Of Mindfulness

Have you ever been so filled up with thoughts that you cannot really concentrate on anything? We have all been there, and when you think of the number of thoughts a human being has a day that is skewed toward negativity, there's a little wonder. The Buddhists allow for mindfulness in their lives because they follow a code, which means that they must behave in certain ways that include things such as concentration and doing things the right way. The right way to them is to be in the moment, and although that doesn't mean much to westerners, it will by the time you have finished reading this chapter.

For the next few minutes, simply sit and do whatever you normally do, but instead of ignoring thoughts, take a look at them and see where they take you. If they take you into situations that have already happened, then you are thinking about the past. If they take you into worrying about the future, then you are placing your mind in the future. Mindfulness takes both of these out of the equation because the past has happened, and nothing you can do can change it, and the future hasn't happened yet. Thus, empty out those thoughts and be here now. For a moment, close your eyes and use your senses to think about the environment you are in. What can you smell? What can you taste? What do you feel? The idea of mindfulness is to make each moment of your life count as a new experience, rather than wasting the moment by spending it either in the past or the future. There are those who believe that multi-tasking is the order of the day in their lives, but the fact is that the parts of the brain that deal with logical thinking can't actually multitask. You may be able to jump quickly from one task to another when this becomes a habit, but the brain won't be processing more than one task at a time, and that's why it's able to respond so quickly when changes occur.

During the course of learning mindfulness, you may be asked to try different things. For example, you may be asked to concentrate on your breathing. A lot of people don't realize the significance of this task. The fact is that most of us don't use the lung capacity that we have because we don't need to in order to stay alive. However, when you breathe correctly, as you are taught later in the book, you actually improve what's going on in your body and systems such as the sympathetic nervous system is able to do its work more efficiently. This system sends blood to muscles and allows you to be active. It's the same system that regulates heat and cold and the human perception of it. There are so many different jobs done by the body that can't be done properly, while breathing is shallow. Thus, the first thing you are taught is to be in the breath – or to concentrate on breathing. When you do things like yoga, breathing comes into it as well because it helps you maximum flexibility for the moves that you are encouraged to do during a yoga session.

Other things you notice when you are mindful are all the things that touch your senses.

Sight

Taste

Touch

Hearing

Smell

You may be able to hear the birds singing outside, or taste that last sip of coffee that you had, or touch the left of a plant or even see cobwebs forming on the bushes in the morning dew. You are conscious of the moment that you are in, and when you are mindful, you notice everything happening around you and are able to stay in that moment without ruining it with unnecessary thought. You may think that this is almost impossible, but the training I will be giving you later in the book will help you to deal with that together with the relaxation exercises that I will explain within its own chapter.

We are not accustomed to the quiet of the mind. In fact, in this day and age, what happens is that we are constantly being interrupted by alerts, by noises around us, by advertising and all manner of things that we think are normal. But, if you can cut out the background noise and get back to feeling silent, you will find that stress will diminish, and your heartbeat will be slower. You will be more conscious of yourself and your relationship with your body and thus learn to live a very peaceful existence even though you cannot imagine this at this point in time.

One of the greatest things about this is the peace that it brings you, but in the early stages, it will take a while to get out of the habit of noise – both from external sources and from the thoughts that you allow to rumble through your mind. The whole basis of mindfulness is to let go and to stop the judgment of people and things so that negative thoughts are kept to a minimum, and you are more comfortable with the thought processes that are going on in your mind – and thus become less stressed by them. It is a recognized fact now by doctors and scientists that this helps you to improve your state of mental health as well as assisting you in staving off the effects of aging and remain mentally active for longer. Mindfulness takes part of its roots from meditation, but bearing in mind the lives that people live in this day and age, it goes further than that in that it takes you back to a time when your senses were used more, and your intuition was sharper. The relationship that you strike up between your mind and your body helps you to stay well and to fight off stress as and when it happens. Does this mean that you avoid your problems? Of course not, but you do learn to become stronger so that you see these problems as stepping stones toward something more important rather than hurdles that give you stress. The compassion that you gain during mindfulness practice means that you are better armed to deal with events in your life that may otherwise be the cause of stress.

Think about it for a moment. There are times in your life when life is indeed difficult. How do you think that an overloaded mind can deal with this? It gets to the point where you can no longer hear your thoughts, you have no clarity of vision and are unable to deal with problems because they become too much of a weight for you to be able to cope with. When you practice mindfulness, you start at the basics and learn to breathe, learn to relax, and learn to empty out all of the garbage that has been accumulating in your mind. You may say that you have always been a person who worries, but there's nothing stopping you from changing. Once you get into a habit of using mindfulness, you find that your mind is capable of dealing with things that you may have thought impossible in the past.

There are different kinds of mindfulness too. Let's look at ways in which you can practice mindfulness:

While doing breathing exercises

While eating

While walking

While bathing

While enjoying the company of friends

While reflecting on the day

While trying to go to sleep

While getting up

It is not about the singularity. It's about peace inside you, and that, in turn, will attract those people who are also positive in their approach to life, so your social life is able to improve with very little input at all. You are more aware of the people around you and more compassionate in your dealings with others. You are kinder to yourself and are using all of the human resources that are available to you in order to face life with the right attitude.

That's what mindfulness is all about, and in a nutshell, it's called "being in the moment" and being able to use all of your senses to make the most of that moment.

So how can mindfulness help you with the above activities? It's simple, actually. If you are doing breathing exercises, you are feeding your body with the right amount of oxygen, but you are also helping your body to receive the right amount of oxygen, which will relax the body and make it feel fresh. You are also adding clarity to your thoughts so that you can tackle the more difficult things that come into your day without as much confusion and difficulty. As far as sleep goes, this is a very important element in your life because it's the time when the body is capable of healing itself. If you use the relaxing techniques that I show you in a future chapter, you will be able to sleep better and won't spend so much time thinking in circles of all the negative things that have happened to you during the course of the day. When waking up to a new day, you will feel less tired and more capable of facing whatever the world throws at you.

Mindfulness is based upon simplicity. It means simplifying your life to the extent that your head is uncluttered. Today we hear a lot about decluttering, but often these books refer to your home. Think of mindfulness as decluttering the mind and thus changing your whole approach and attitude toward life.

You will find that relationships will improve because you take more time to listen, and your mind is slow enough to enjoy relationships instead of always seeing them in a negative manner. The compassion that you gain toward other people through mindfulness helps you to drop the concept of criticism and start to adopt the concept of compassion and understanding. Thus you are not as judgmental, and this makes you a nicer person to be with. We are all too quick to criticize and judge others, but mindfulness puts judgment into its rightful place, and you begin to cherish your friendships and be more attentive to people who need you or even people who shower you with their love that may otherwise be taken for granted.

In a future chapter, I am going to get you to go through a relaxation technique. The relaxation and breathing exercises are very necessary before you go headlong into mindfulness meditation. These help to prepare you, so don't think that there are shortcuts. There are no shortcuts to becoming the best person that you can be, but at the end of the day, you will certainly see a different you emerge. There are also exercises in mindfulness on its own, and this can help you to become a more positive person and to make the most of the experiences you have in your life. As for inner strength, you will find that through the use of mindfulness meditation, but you will also find that your intuition is better honed and that you will begin to enjoy all of the human senses that you were born with, instead of taking them for granted and forget what they are there for. There are also health benefits to Mindfulness Meditation, and the next chapter will interest you if this is what you need in order to persuade you to take part.

Chapter 11: Stress

Stress

A popular cause of most of the stress in this world is the sense that an individual is not in control of their own lives. They are in constant fear of not being in the driver seat on the ride of their life journey.

We all know that fear can definitely cause an extreme amount of anxiety because you know that you are not in control of your whole life, and that alone can be very stressful.

Stress is different for all of us; there is not a number one way to define or describe it. There has also never been a perfect way to deal with it, only successful ways to manage it.

It can be hard to regain a sense of control over that, but this is what you must focus on doing to regain control of your life. This will change everything in terms of those negative emotions, and it will change that stress into self-confidence.

Because you are now focused and aware of what needs to be done, what's important and what is not important. No, we are not able to control the events of the world or circumstances that we end up in, but we can control our reactions and how we respond to situations that we may end up in.

Make a list of all the things that really make you angry and cause you daily stress, then decide which ones you can and cannot do something about. There are all types of different ways. This is just one way to get started just a tip like I said for beginners who are not used to dealing with this or not used to journaling or focusing on self-help. Write it down you - will get used to hearing that term over and over. Write it down!

Make sure you set personal boundaries; this is definite protection against daily stress that will take discipline and commitment to make sure that those boundaries are not crossed.

But it will be worth it because it will becomes a habit for you and then you do not actually have to think about doing it. It is just natural once you practice it for a while, so stay committed to your daily practice; it is going to pay off soon.

Some people have stress levels that are so high that they are not mentally prepared to work through these types of things on their own, so they require help from professionals, and that is fine as long as you are aware that that what you need. It is a good sign for someone to seek the help necessary to get them back on track.

But not everyone needs professional help; a lot of times we can work through stress ourselves with these simple steps. It just takes commitment and discipline.

Stress Checklist

*Are you always hiding what you truly think or feel because you do not want other people's opinions, or you might be afraid of their reactions? - You have got to learn to speak your truth and stop worrying about what the outcome will be.

That causes tremendous stress anxiety as well as depression, and it messes with your self-esteem. The following is a checklist for you to see were some of your stress is coming from.

Do you fear that letting people in and letting them know what you are doing will make them criticize you or use it against you later?

Do you only focus on the negative things, violent movies, violent videos, instead of normal and loving things?

Are you afraid to ask for things in your relationship because you are constantly being told you are too demanding, or you think they will ask what is wrong with you?

Do you feel comfortable actually addressing your partner with your needs and wants?

Do you have friends, family, or a partner that is always denying you, degrading you, or putting you down?

Does your point of view matter to the people around you?

Are you constantly made to feel like you can never do anything right?

And you cannot possibly feel good or be fulfilled because if you were self-confident, you would not have a problem asking for what you want or speaking your truth. This is something we need to have you work on immediately.

These are all things that cause heavy amounts of stress because anytime you are walking around carrying fear and pressure about something, it is going to cause you to be stressed!

Do you notice a pattern of disrespect from:

Family members

Friends

Your Partner

Your Co-Workers

Tracklist

Start keeping track of how many times a day you state things like "I'm stressed", "I'm annoyed" or "I'm angry", "I'm hurt" or whatever it may be that you're allowing other people to make you feel or are bringing on yourself. Just start keeping track of how many times a day you say things like this.

Once you do this for a couple of weeks you're going to look at this list that you made and you are going to start to analyze it and realize how ridiculous some of the things are that you allow people to stress you out about or upset you about. It's the same with yourself; most of the things that you stress yourself out about are not even stress worthy.

You are not going to analyze and prioritize; this is where you are going to learn how to separate yourself from a lot of that stress that is so unnecessary because you are going to realize most of the stuff is silly and very unimportant.

This is a very special exercise because it will reveal to you the things that are not in line with the values of your life. First of all, once you study this list and analyze it, you are going to feel silly and it is going to make you laugh. Many of these things happen to you on a regular basis, and now you can actually look at them on paper and laugh at them.

You have mastered the concept of anticipating situations before they even happen, but they will not stress you out any longer because you are aware of them and have decided not to waste your energy.

Even if you did think it was a stressful situation or stressful person, you have decided that it is not going to take your energy anymore. You already know ahead of time who gets on your nerves at work, who annoys you, who you do not want to be around, so you can automatically manage your stress level.

You know that already, so decide early in the morning who or what is not going to bother you that day and you are going to look at them and laugh. Yes, they are still going to irritate you, but the effect is going to be on a totally different level, as if you are outside of the irritation instead of being consumed by it.

Self-Control & Self-Discipline

Self-control can be learned, practiced, and mastered by anyone who desires to achieve it.

Gaining awareness, practice, commitment, repetition, and plenty of hard work; the payoff is well worth it, and that is going to be your success.

You can achieve a lot with more self-control, including higher self-esteem, less depression, better time management, the ability to manage your emotions, and you will become more reliable and trustworthy.

Just like another muscle in your body, the more you use it, the more you exercise with it, the stronger, it's going to get. Know that you have this muscle and make mental notes of the fact that you are working every day to make it stronger. It takes consistent practicing of your mental energy to make tough decisions that involve self-control, skillful planning, strategic thinking, and being certain that things are done correctly.

Change negative or self-defeating thoughts into positive ideas and be consistent in doing what is right when you are supposed to, and avoid things that you are not supposed to do. These are all simple everyday exercises that you can do to strengthen your self-control and self-discipline.

Waiting to obtain or experience something until a later time, taking charge of what you say, do and think are all ways of improving your self-control. Reaching your goals will require you to have an extreme amount of self-discipline as well.

When you stay focused on being positive, helping others, doing what is right, keeping your house clean, telling the truth, showing compassion for yourself and others, it will help you to keep your energy in the correct place. This will result in extremely good self-control.

Just A Few Benefits of Self-Control:

More positive outcomes

More of a calm presence

Healthy & loving relationships

Stress-Free

Constant success with achieving goals

Peaceful and fulfilled life

Our brains are trying to make our thoughts real, so you need to make sure that your thoughts are set on positive memories, situations, dreams, accomplishments, emotions, and people. Another important key to gaining strong self-control is not to try and change the feeling that you are experiencing at that moment or pretend that it does not exist.

The proper way to deal with that is to face the emotion head-on, acknowledge it, feel it, and release it. You are feeling the emotions without allowing them to grab hold of you and lock you down in the basement of anxiety, self-pity, anger, or depression.

Dealing with difficult situations and circumstances as well as irritating people can be a very constructive way of testing the strength of your self-control. You will get better at dealing with and being around these people when you absolutely need to. Especially when you are dealing with those people who are the most challenging, difficult, or annoying. It can also assist you in becoming more productive in your relationships because you understand how to control your emotions.

You will also become a better leader, student, team player thinker, and winner.

You should begin to think carefully about everything that you say and all of the actions that you take; you will be sure to make careful decisions.

Tips to keep in mind while working on your self-control & self-discipline:

Use your power

Be aware of emotions at all times

Resist dangerous urges

Slow down

Be prepared

Be Proactive

Show compassion

Stay true to yourself

Keep a humble spirit

Chapter 12: The Concept Of Deliberate Thinking

How many times a day have you literally stopped to think about the topic and subject of breathing? Even though you do it every second of your life? As long as you are still alive, that is. Some-thing as important and vital as our living, breathing self, yet it never really crosses our minds to automatically put it on the top of our "gratitude list" to be thankful we are able to breathe with ease today, right? Well if you did, then congratulations, you are a blessed being who have mastered the art of being grateful for the little things in life that literally gave life to you.

When you have a practiced mind, you will naturally become a very selective sifter of your own thoughts. You will not miss a single opportunity that comes through the cracks, to feel thankful for, and in our meditative practice, what better ways than to pick our breath to do it? When you gather all of your focus and concentration and direct it to breathing in a manner where the rhythm and timing of it soothe you, it will gradually get easier to be still and not find yourself (your mind) wandering about carelessly.

You will be "in tuned", "aligned", and "in harmony" with your breath, and as you practice daily consistently, you will start to enjoy that quality time set aside just to concentrate on your breath. It is the best way to start off having something to focus on to quiet the mind and using the breath is effective because it makes audible noises (but not overbearing) and you have complete control over it to exaggerate the way you breathe to the degree it holds your attention for periods long enough to stay focused throughout your practice.

Therefore, deliberate breathing equates to deliberate thinking. You pay attention to it on purpose and then proceed to use it as a tool to serve you directly and intentionally. You will see instant results. The more focused and concentrated you are, the less you feel distracted or feel the need to fidget physically while you are "meditating". Meditation comes in many different forms and ways. Some people verbally chant sutras, and play music that will guide them through that whole 20-30 minutes, some find other forms of outlets to ensure that quality time was set aside to focus on themselves. As long as it takes your attention for at least a full 20-30 minutes without interruption and allows you, to focus on you, that is meditating.

You have to keep in mind, each practice does not need to be categorized into a "good" or "bad" attempt. Your own practice is for the sole purpose of completely honoring and loving yourself, therefore, you can't evaluate it as you would do a performance. If you carry this mindset of "grading" yourself with you, it will entirely write off the actual purposeful intention of it, and if there's any goal to these practices, it is very simply–to learn. It is the quickest route to mastery and growth when you take a "learning mind" with you. If the time goes by and you forget or miss your practices, just "forgive" and "restart" again.

That is the very first step towards accepting yourself. Each time you feel like you fall below your own bars and standards you've set, don't beat yourself up and wallow in self-pity and just acknowledge your small efforts and baby steps you have taken. It matters how you approach the subject because the way you handle forgiveness towards yourself is the way you would apply to others around you, even if you don't know it just yet.

You'll be imperfect at this, but that's okay. Investigate what have thrown you off course, learn from it, then in that space of self-awareness, you create a new opportunity to "invite" yourself to begin again. "Letting yourself in" is the first big step you take in learning to have full acceptance of your freedom to make mistakes and understanding they are not flaws, but rather, personal attempts to try something new. You will eventually get the hang of it if your heart is set on mastering it; whatever it may be.

Chapter 13: The Value Of Mindfulness

Mindfulness has a strong impact on your ability to transform your life and get all that you desire from it. When you are mindful, you open yourself up to the ability to make the internal changes that are necessary for you to acquire the external changes that you desire. Although it appears to be a very spiritual practice, mindfulness is actually a very logical and strategic practice that enables you to unlock many opportunities in life.

Mindfulness is brought up in many areas of life, both spiritual and nonspiritual. You may realize that many extremely successful people, including most billionaires, have included mindfulness into their life. That is because when you are mindful, you are highly focused on what you want in your life and therefore you make decisions that only assist you in attracting those things into your life, nothing else. Often times when we don't practice mindfulness, we end up making decisions that are not focused on our inner most wants, desires and needs. As a result, we end up not having what it is that we want in life because we have not been mindful about our actions in attracting it. In the past when you have made decisions that you deemed were wrong, you likely realize now that at the time, you had been acting out of emotion. The most common emotion we react from, instead of respond from, is stress. When we are stressed out we act with emotion in a way that is not clearly aimed towards our specific wants or needs in life. Because of this, we may end up actually pushing away what we want and need, instead of drawing it in closer.

Throughout this book, you are going to see a lot of references to Buddhism and Dharma. These teachings offer powerful insights into the way of life and how you can lead a mindful and happy life in general. It is important to realize that these teachings are not exactly a religion, but rather a way of life. Buddhism and Dharma teachings offer a perspective-based study on life without you necessarily having to worship any Gods. As Albert Einstein said: "If there is any religion that could correspond to the needs of modern science, it would be Buddhism."

As you read this book you are going to learn about many ways that you can use mindfulness in your life and how it can powerfully transform your life as a result of your actions. You should make sure that you keep an open mind throughout this process. As much as it may seem so, mindfulness is actually as much practical and logical as it is spiritual. Because of that, you do not necessarily need to be a spiritual or religious person in any way, shape or form in order to use mindfulness and benefit from all that it has to offer.

If you have been struggling to practice mindfulness up until now, it may be because you are leading a lifestyle or carrying habits that present as obstacles to the process of mindfulness. Many times, we have a lifestyle that keeps us reacting out of emotion or simply carrying out mindless activities based on old routines and habits we have built into our lives. These old outdated habits and routines can actually deviate away from our ability to be mindful and our ability to gain value from mindfulness itself. It is important that you learn to start recognizing these obstacles and pay attention so you can find out exactly how you can overcome them and carry on in your mindfulness journey.

When you lead a mindful life, there is so much more to it than just being in a Zen state or doing meditation on a regular basis. Mindfulness is a mental state that you achieve and balance throughout your life as a means to remove as much emotional baggage as you possibly can so that you can free yourself from it. As a result of this freeing activity, you open yourself up to the ability to have an extremely clear mind that will allow you to make every decision and action thoughtfully, instead of acting in reaction to thoughts, emotions or fleeting feelings that you experience.

Knowing that mindfulness is a state of mind that you must achieve and balance, it may become overwhelming to you. This is especially true if you try to achieve mindfulness all in one go, as it can take a lot of work to achieve it. For some, it is even impossible to achieve a mindful state all in one go. The best way for you to do it is to take your time and start becoming mindful of a few things at a time, and working your way up to a totally mindful state of life. For those who try to go too fast, you may discover that it is too hard to face and let go of that much emotional baggage at once, and you may end up feeling worse off as a result. It is best to take your time and focus on what matters most and then work your way up from there.

If you are a more logical based mind, it may help you to understand that Buddhism and Dharma teachings are the best scientific way emotional behavior to for human psychology and

be explained to the average person. Through these teachings, you can learn why humans take certain positive or negative psychological and physical based actions and reactions to certain triggers. While the messages can sometimes seem cryptic, they are often easily translatable into something that will allow you to take a realistic and honest look at yourself and apply it in a practical way that will allow you to get closer to the state of total mindfulness.

Chapter Summary:

• Mindfulness is a state of mind that can help you transform your life
• When you are mindful, you are not operating from an emotional state
• Keeping an open mind about this book will help you gain maximum value

- Buddhism and Dharma offer the best teachings about mindfulness
- Buddhism and Dharma are a way of life
- You cannot achieve a mindful state all at once

Chapter 14: Mindfulness Meditation

Mindfulness literally means "to be aware of something", or to pay attention, but to what? To the present, to here and now in our life. Mindfulness goal is to be aware of being, of your own ego without any judgement, to simply living in harmony with ourselves and with anything that surrounds us, in this exact moment of our life. This leads the life state of a person to rise, and to a better wellness for our mind.

Becoming aware and no longer critical and severe towards ourselves or towards our life, we can control our negative energies, or better said, we can control our negative emotions, sensations and thoughts. Through mindfulness we can detach ourselves from the reality that surrounds us, observing from above, in a rational and objective way, our existence and our being in the universe which surrounds us. This modern technique, based on psychological studies, is a treatment used for different pathologies to improve mind perception, consequently obtaining benefits on a physical, mental and creative level.

As is often the case, these psychophysical improvement techniques derive from antique holistic disciplines, which have been part of our world for thousands of years. In fact, mindfulness has a Buddhist background, which does not include the religious sphere.

Mindfulness is a meditation technique aimed to the research for self-consciousness, which in the Buddhist tradition is called the Samma Sati, which in Pali language means the "right consciousness". Specifically, this concept comes from the Theravada Buddhist current, which is based on the Four Noble Truths of Shakyamuni Buddha and on the elaboration of life, of Zen and other practices like yoga. The stressful life we live nowadays constantly brings negative thoughts into our minds, that eventually lead to anxiety, depression and emotional distress. All these mechanisms of self-criticism and self-blame generate an infinite vortex of negative energy which, accumulated in our inner self, explodes in all aspects of our life. Training ourselves with mindfulness we allow our mind to transform that negative energy, which deteriorates our body and our ego, rediscovering positivity and joy.

Therapist so helps people to change their perception of their thoughts, the relationship with the mental contents. Too often indeed much of the suffering we built up in our lives comes from the complexity of our thoughts. If our thinking is more fluid and positive then our mind will be quieter. Mindfulness meditation is practiced in the same way of traditional meditation, sitting cross-legged and with closed eyes, concentrating on one's breath channeled into the abdomen, which is the diaphragmatic breath. Diaphragmatic breath is the natural and ideal breath of our organism. Normally we breath with our chest not allowing us to let all the air enter the lungs, as it happens instead when we breathe using the diaphragm. Thanks to diaphragmatic breath our body relaxes, blowing off steam from the neck to the shoulders, assuming a correct and straight position and bettering our voice tone.

Observing the way we breath we can understand a lot about our physical and emotional state, since a person who is in a state of anxiety will find himself breathing heavily with his chest, sometimes jumping his breath and feeling deprived of air; on the contrary a relaxed person will breathe with his diaphragm and will have a calm and peaceful breathing. But how do you breath with your diaphragm? If we have never tried it before, let's start lying down in a supine position, observing our abdomen that swells while we breathe in through the nose; then, after holding the breath for a few seconds, let's throw the air out of the mouth. To correctly breathe with the diaphragm a lot of practice is required, so keep it up!

Mindfulness practice embraces all aspects of our life, so after this introduction, made to better understand the topic we are dealing with, practical examples will be illustrated to learn how to get this self-awareness we have spoken so much about, to manage stress and anxiety and to achieve inner peace with ourselves. The topics will go from meditation to physical exercise, moving then on feeding and on introducing children into this beautiful experience.

Going back to mediations, they are quite short at the beginning, about 10 minutes, then they increase with time and experience. Meditating every day and with regularity, the attention that is initially placed on the breath will then be placed also on thoughts, words and actions. This program in turn, on the base of the great success on patients, has given rise to other programs such as Mindfulness Based Cognitive Therapy, whose goal is to help patients to totally transform their relationship with their thoughts, their emotions and their physical sensations. This meditative therapy is suitable for everyone, starting with children (Evolution Mindfulness), up to the older people. In addition to group activities, sessions or retreats, there are practical aspects of this philosophy that can be applied every day and in every moment of our lives.

Chapter 15: Practicing Mindfulness

Mindlessness is the characteristic of human life, but there is no need to worry because there are ways to cultivate mindfulness. Remember, mindfulness is all about being aware of the present experience and accepting things as they are. We feel depression when things don't go the way we want and think that we could control the events. We must realize that we cannot control all the events and we cannot dictate every event in life. We have to develop the habit of accepting the reality with an open heart.

Learning Mindfulness

There are some informal and some formal meditation techniques which you can practice for the cultivation of mindfulness. It is not impossible, but it takes seriousness and consistency. First of all, you need to ask yourself "am I ready to start it now"? Next, tell yourself that you need to concentrate on these practices if you want good results.

- Focus

The focus is the key to mindfulness practices. It is just like focusing the lens while taking a picture. In this case, train your mind to focus like a lens. For concentration and focus, a common principle applies. Choose an object and then:

Ø Keep the object on a table or a stool.

Ø Sit in a chair and watch the object.

Ø Keep watching for 5 minutes and next day increase this time to 10 minutes and keep increasing the timing through the coming days.

Not something strange because this practice is well known and accepted across the whole world, mostly owing to the telepathic adventurers. Once you train your mind to focus on an object, test your mind's ability to focus on other things (visible and invisible). These things may include a particular sound, a feeling of sensation, and a word spoken or written.

For mindfulness practices, make sure that you have at least 30 minutes during which nothing is going to distract you.

Breath Awareness

Breath Awareness is our first mindfulness cultivation meditation exercise. Simply sit in a chair or on anything you feel comfortable. Make sure that the back of the chair keeps your spine straight. Now just create a feeling that a string is attached to your forehead and raise your forehead towards the ceiling (raise your forehead slowly until you feel yourself in a comfortable posture). Rest your hands on your knees and sit as still as you can. The idea is to keep the mind alert and body, relaxed. Then close your eyes and then pay attention to your breath. What you need is to concentrate on the sensation caused by the breath. The best point is the rise and fall of the tummy. Focus your mind on the rise and fall of the tummy while keeping the eyes closed during this whole exercise. Slowly, try to feel every body part involved in the process of the inhale and exhale. Track this cycle through your mind. Do not worry about the breathing speed because this exercise is for concentration not for breath-control.

Do not worry if other thoughts distract because it is normal and you cannot avoid it in the first attempt. You must slowly bring the mind back to the breathing sensation, as soon as you realize the distraction. It is just as a pet owner, stopping the puppy from wandering away. Just as a good owner does not panic, you need to stay calm and direct your mind slowly and mildly. There is no room for panic or anything done in a hurry because it will ruin the whole exercise.

As your eyes are closed, how are you going to keep track of the time? Well, 20 minutes is just for naming a time limit. There is no hard and fast rule for this time setting. You may stretch this exercise to beyond 30 minutes or keep it for 12 to 15 minutes, but the idea is to concentrate and entirely focus during the training.

When the exercise is over, try to replace the breath with something else, a sound, birds chirp or anything else. Keep changing this selection with the passage of time. You may choose multiple focus points at a time, and it works well in the long run.

The next stage is to focus on different sensations, increase the focus points and practice this exercise every day. Within a week, the results will start to bring fruit. You'll realize that your mind is in a better state to experience the happenings in the surroundings. This is what mindfulness requires, beware of the present, and accept the existence of these things.

A Mindful Life

Once you learn to concentrate, in fact, train your mind to concentrate, start applying this ability in everyday life. When you focus on things around you, your mind will not distract, and there will be less room for the worries to create fearful feelings about future. The whole idea is to allow yourself live in reality and enjoy life as it presents itself.

Once again, keep telling your mind that you are not responsible for whatever is happening. There is no need of blaming your life for the events. The important aspect is to stay satisfied or at least free from sorrowful grief.

Think practically. Suppose you have some tools and you want to build something using those tools. Rather than dreaming about what tools you lack, it is vital to think about the way you can use the tools you have. Same is the case with our life. We must learn to stay happy with the resources we have and make full use of the existing resources rather than worrying about what we lack or worrying about the possible troubles in the future.

Fears kill us too early even before the fearsome events take place. In the next chapter, we are going to learn how to deal with the fears, anxiety and worries and importance of visualizing the light in the dark.

Chapter 16: What Is Mindfulness?

According to Juliet Adams, the founder of Mindfulnet.org and a director at A Head for Work, the ABC of mindfulness is:

A – AWARENESS – to become aware of what you are doing and what you are thinking, of what is going on around you, in your body and in your mind;

B – BEING – or "just being" with your own experiences; to avoid being on autopilot and to avoid feeding your problems by creating a story of your own

C – SEEING - for seeing what is going on and to respond in a wiser manner, by creating gaps between what happens and how you react to it

Mindfulness is a form of meditation that, until recent years, was almost unheard of in the West. Typically, meditation involves you focusing all of your attention entirely on your breath, as you breathe in and out. Doing this lets you "watch" your thoughts as they come to the forefront of your mind and, as time goes by, you will learn how to see them without struggling. You will begin to realize that your thoughts will always be there, that they will come and they will go all by themselves; you are not your thoughts and learning how to be mindful will allow you to separate your thoughts from you.

You will learn to see your thoughts appear, from out of nowhere and you will learn to see them disappear again, without weighing heavily on you. You will come to the understanding that all your feelings, your thoughts, even the negative ones are transient, that they come and then they go. The most important thing you will learn is that you have the ultimate choice as to whether you act on those thoughts and feelings or let them slide past you.

Mindfulness is all about being observant without being critical. When you find yourself weighed down by stress or unhappiness, instead of taking it to heart, you will learn to treat that stress and unhappiness as if they were nothing more than black clouds above you in the sky, and you will learn to see those clouds as something of mild curiosity, something to glance at as they drift past you. Mindfulness is all about catching all of those negative thought patterns before they weigh you down and push you into a downward spiral. Mindfulness is about taking back complete control of your life.

Over the course of time, provided you practice mindfulness regularly, it will start to bring long-term changes to your life in terms of your well being, your happiness levels, and your moods. There have been plenty of scientific studies carried out on mindfulness and they show that it cannot only stop depression, it can also have a positive effect on your day-to-day brain patterns, on how you cope with stress and anxiety, depression, irritability so that, when you begin to feel that way, those feelings dissolve quickly. There are other studies that have shown that those who meditate regularly tend to visit their doctor far less often and will, over the course of time, spend less time in hospital. Their memory is vastly improved, their levels of creativity rise and they can react much faster. However, despite all of this being proved, people are still a little on the wary side when they hear about meditation so, to help you along the way, I have decided to smash a few of the more, shall we say, common of the myths that surround mindfulness meditation:

Myth 1 – Meditation is religious; I'm not.

Fact – Meditation has nothing whatsoever to do with religion. It is simply a way of training your mind and, although many religious people do meditate, so do many agnostics and atheists.

Myth 2 – You have to sit cross-legged. How do I do that at work?

Fact – You do not need to sit cross-legged to meditate! Obviously, you can if you want to but the most important thing is that you are comfortable. Many people meditate sitting on a chair, while on the bus or the train, even while walking to the shops or work. Meditation is not about going into a trance, it is about becoming aware of your surroundings and you can meditate pretty much anywhere.

Myth 3 – Meditation takes too much time - time I just don't have.

Fact - Mindfulness meditation does not take a great deal of time, only persistence and patience. When you first start learning to meditate, obviously it will take longer but, eventually, you will find that you can meditate over a 10-minute coffee break. Most people who learn mindfulness meditation soon find that they have more time than they ever thought possible because meditation frees them from time pressures.

Myth 4 – Meditation is hard to learn; I won't be able to do it.

Fact – meditation is not hard to learn and you must never see it as something that you must succeed at or that you will fail it – that is not what it is about. Even when you find it difficult to meditate, you are still learning about how your mind works and you have still gained the benefits.

Myth 5 – Meditation will deaden my mind and I won't be able to move forward in my life

Fact – The absolute last thing that mindfulness meditation does is deaden your mind. In fact, it will have the opposite effect of freshening your mind up. Meditation is not about acceptance of things that are not acceptable; it is about seeing things more clearly so that you can make informed decisions, take better actions to change what needs changing. Meditation is all about cultivating a deep awareness, more compassion that allows you to see what your goals are and find the right path towards them.

In the next chapter, I will talk more about the benefits of mindfulness meditation before we look at how to do it.

Chapter 17: What Is Mindfulness?

Add chaAccording to one of the masters of meditation, John Cabazon, mindfulness is an act of purposely paying attention on present while not making any judgment on the present moment; being observant of the inner feelings and thought without reacting or running away fro it

When you practice mindfulness you don't replay the past. You don't concentrate on what has already happened, but rather on the present moment and its sensation

To be really honest, Mindfulness's true origination comes from the word Awareness. It's where you are seeing the thing as it is without any judgment.

Here is the next definition that John Cabazon uses It's like paying attention on purpose.

What does purpose here means?

Purpose

Let's take that example of eating and look at it a bit further. When we are purposefully aware of eating, we are consciously being aware of the process of eating. We're deliberately noticing the sensations and our responses to those sensations. We're noticing the mind wandering, and when it does wander we purposefully bring our attention back.

Another example:

In the present moment, If we look, very carefully and slowly Mind keeps on playing the past over, and then it is projecting the near future for no reason. It is never in the present.and with that emotional turbulence.

How to be Non-judgmental. towards thoughts and fellings?

It's like being a watcher like Eagle; for example, the Night watchmen like in "Game of Thrones" don't worry I will explain better ahead. When practicing mindfulness, we are not aiming to suppress or control or even stop our thoughts and feelings. We are simply paying attention to our experiences without labeling them good or bad

Mindfulness then allows us to become the watcher of our perception of our senses, thoughts, and emotions as they arise, without being caught in them and being ripped away in the current. And that's POWER.

By becoming the watcher in this way, we are less likely to play out the old habits of thinking and live and make excellent decisions in life or at least increase its probability.

How Do You Practice Mindfulness?

I believe there are two ways, active and passive mindfulness.

Have you ever noticed that when you are fully involved in something, it's as if you are lost in it. Example playing your favorite sports or watching your favorite TV show..

I believe it's called active mindfulness, where you are not bothered, You are so glad and happy no thought are present there is nothing It's absolute peace and joy its also non as flow .

Then, there is passive mindfulness.

It's like recharging ourselves. this is the reason people get into meditation and mindfulness,. It's like when we are buried under negative emotions and thoughts or negative patterns.

Here you simply put down your inner Armor and knowledge of the past and bring every emotion and though of the past on your breath and observe it and let go by putting our attention on breath observe it it will go in the background,this is called passive mindfulness which people are mostly interested in.

What Can Mindfulness Do for You?

If you all have come this far, I would like to congratulate you facts show 80% don't go through books first pages. you are different believe it to become different in true sense.

Chapter 18: What Is Mindfulness?

Most people do not have real direction in life and many wonder what their real purpose in life is. These thoughts can make you become depressed and unhappy thus affecting your relationships, career and even your health due to the stress you experience.

More people are seeking to make positive changes in their life by investing in mindfulness exercises training, a powerful way of achieving complete life fulfillment.

Most people have no idea what mindfulness exercises training or therapy really is so here we will give you some insight on its benefits and theories. If you want to make a positive change in your life then you can make a start today by investing in the course that involved brain training on a deep subconscious level.

Mindfulness exercises therapy will clarify many areas of your life and can be considered a form of life coaching. Often meditation comes as part of the course a very necessary exercise to calm the spirit train the mind and relieve stress.

Mindfulness training helps you handle problems and difficult situations more effectively because you will be able to think clearly, calmly and make calculated decisions.

Another important benefit of mindfulness exercises training helps you find a proper balance in all areas of your life. For example a career can become an all consuming demand thus making you neglect family, recreation, and health issues. Break bad habits become more creative and enjoy the beauty of life around you by being mindful.

Mindfulness is a way of seeing life clearly, understanding what your purpose in life is clarifying goals you want to achieve and having a deeper understanding on an emotional level and spiritual level.

Do you want to break bad habits, live a healthier life, reduce stress and live life to the fullest in every moment of the present?

If you answer yes to all of these questions, then mindfulness training is an incredible investment to fix all areas of your life. Seek proper courses for mind fullness training and this way you will allow the experts show you how to start living a happier healthier more fulfilled life, loving relationships and balance.

Mind training often called mindfulness training can open many doors in your life. Few people understand how powerful the subconscious in and that you can rewire it to attract wealth, health, and overall well being and access. The sensible way to learn mindfulness exercises is by combining with meditation and even Yoga from the masters.

Mindfulness exercises using meditation and the help of audio can allow you to retrain your mind. Transcendental

Meditation can be done anywhere and will produce a deep state of peace calmness and relaxation. Learning meditation basics is easier with the help of audio and this is a first step in mindfulness exercises.

Once you have mastered mind control you can map your life into fulfillment choosing for tranquility, peace and harmony even though the world around you is swirling with fast paced technologies and noise.

Mindfulness exercises will help you eliminate jumbled thoughts and help you concentrate while reducing stress. The result is enhanced physical and emotional well being. Invest in meditation videos and music, a course in Yoga, programs in mind training and subconscious management and they will definitely change your life.

Mindfulness exercises come with many life coaching programs because without proper mind training you can be adrift in chaos and disorder. Stress in our daily lives has many additional mental frames of mind that come with it all damaging your inner peace. Aggression, frustration, impatience, and depression can all be caused by stress. Mindfulness exercises with meditation will help you break the chains holding you back so consider it worth any investment you make!

Chapter 19: Welcome

You may be wondering exactly what this Mindfulness is all about. Our experts, Franne and Dana have provided some excellent insight.

Dana said, "To me, mindfulness is the purposeful practice of being present to what is happening within me and around me. It is a neutral observation and acceptance of what is - without censoring, judging, commenting, comparing, or needing it to be different. When my mind begins to engage in those activities, I simply choose to bring my awareness back to my breath, back to the present moment, back to whatever it is that I am focused on in that moment."

Franne said, "Mindfulness means attentiveness. When I am mindful I pay attention to my surroundings, my **self** and my process, and those around me. I am "tuning" in instead of "tuning out". I am witnessing and I am engaged." Franne also said that she started doing Mindfulness because she uses it to cultivate a deep sense of compassion and presence. You may be wondering what compassion and presence has to do with stress, anxiety and worry. Truthfully, all I can tell you is you will understand after you've practiced Mindfulness. The compassion that Franne talks about isn't only concerning other people. You will also develop a compassion for **yourself**. If you realize it or not, you deserve that, and you need it as well.

Take a nice, long breath in through your nose… and blow out your air through your mouth. Imagine yourself living your life with no anxiety or worry, and see yourself responding to stress in a positive, relaxed way. Take another long breath in through your nose and then exhale through your mouth and really see this in your mind. When you're ready, continue reading.

After practicing mindfulness, what you just imagined will be your new reality.

You may have realized that in the above visualization, you did not picture your life with NO stress. That is because stress is inevitable; but how you **deal** with stress is open to change. Right now, when a major (or even not so major) stress comes into your life, you react strongly. After all, stress builds up over time and can become a huge mountain in front of you. And that huge mountain can have boulders rolling down them. And then, when any new stressor presents itself, it is easy to overreact and spin out of control.

The key to dealing with stress is to know how to approach it calmly. Simply stated – Mindfulness will allow you to approach stress calmly.

When it comes to anxiety and worry, Mindfulness will allow them to be a thing of the past. In basic terms, Mindfulness allows you to focus on the present moment. The "now". Not the future. Not the past. Right now. Well, anxiety and worry live someplace else besides right **now**.

Believe me; I fully understand feeling anxious/worried. Actually, it all starts with worry and then can quickly escalate to anxiety. It's because of all of the thoughts going on in your mind. The "what if's" sneak in. The bad scenarios play out... It is a horrible predicament to be in; but when you practice Mindfulness, it will teach you to be in the moment. When you are in the moment, you appreciate what is happening right here and now and you won't even allow yourself to step off that slippery, worrisome, anxious edge.

I would like to take a moment to welcome you to a new way of life. Your family and friends are going to wonder what has happened in your life to create the person that you are about to become.

If you will commit to a regular Mindfulness practice (don't worry, it's not a long time each day), you will notice benefits of being mindful very quickly. Even after your first Mindfulness experience.

Wanna jump in and see what it's all about? Do you have three minutes? That's right. Three minutes.

Would you like to know a little bit of what to expect? First and foremost – thoughts will come to your mind! Mindfulness is not about controlling your mind. You are not controlling the fact that thoughts are "not supposed" to enter your mind. You are going to **allow** those thoughts to come; but when they do, notice them as a thought, and then let them drift away. You can either send them on their way by imagining them as balloons, or watching them drift away on a cloud, down a river, or out to sea. The choice is yours. It's totally fine for those thought to come; but when they do, bid them farewell and imagine them leaving. After you watch those thoughts leave, re-focus on your breathing.

The second part to this simple Mindfulness session is to notice YOU during the Mindfulness. Your breathing. The way your clothes rub against your skin when you breathe. The temperature of the air on your skin. Small noises happening around you. The way your feet feel, and the way your body feels. Just **notice**.

The last part is simply not to judge yourself. When thoughts come, fine. Let them come and watch them leave. Maybe you'll find yourself overthinking about something you notice. That's fine. It's just a thought. Watch it leave. No judgement. You are wonderful, and how ever you do this mindfulness time, is perfect for you.

This is what Dana said about her thoughts, "The biggest challenge has been not judging myself for having negative, limiting, or judgmental thoughts. Even after 20 something years of personal and spiritual development, I still have these kinds of thoughts. Thankfully, I don't have them very often and I am rarely triggered by them. When I do have them, I just notice them, and allow myself to be ok with them. As a result, I have learned to be kinder and more compassionate with myself."

Here is what you do:

Go someplace quiet. There is no shame in hiding out on the toilet if that is the only place you can get some quiet.

Set an alarm for 3 minutes. (This way you won't have to worry about how much time you have left.)

Take a conscious breath in through your nose and exhale through your mouth. Do this 2 times.

Allow yourself to start noticing the way you're breathing, the way your clothes feel on your skin. The way your body feels wherever you are sitting or lying. Allow thoughts to come; but then usher them out. Notice them as thoughts and let them go. Refocus on your breathing…

Before you know it, your timer will ding.

There will be obstacles when you first start. That is completely normal and to be expected. After all, you have spent so much time in a world of stress, anxiety and worry.

When asked, Dana had the following to say about obstacles when first starting out:

"At first it was just sitting still and not being distracted by my body. Then the challenge was allowing myself to be present to all of my thoughts – the good, the bad, and the ugly – without judging the thoughts, or myself for having the thoughts. Then my practice focused on being more mindful in all areas of my life. This is still my practice today. The breath is always my focus. It brings me back to the present moment and whatever I am doing in that moment. The only thing I struggle with now is making time for a regular, seated meditation practice. Recently I let this go, to make time for my writing, and it is my intention to bring it back again, to make time for both."

Franne added this, "Mindfulness requires intention and the decision to work at cultivating it as a habit or way of being. It's so easy to lose that intention when the challenges of life show up. For me to overcome the distractions of life and pull back to my center I do my best to surround myself with conscious people who are also on a path toward mindful living."

As I am sure you noticed in the simple Mindfulness exercise above, you had quite a bit of mind chatter, or thoughts that would pop into your head. There are times, when the chatter gets too much that Franne will simply abandon her meditation and try it again at a later time; but then again, there are times that she will simply keep going and let it be what it is. Dana will focus on her breath, repeat a mantra, or use some other technique to calm her mind. Sometimes she will even say, "STOP" out loud. When she keeps redirecting her awareness, the chatter and thoughts will slow down to the point where she will still be aware of them; but not triggered by them anymore.

Welcome to Mindfulness. Now, are you ready to change your life?

Chapter 20: How To Practice Mindfulness

There are endless ways that you can be more mindful throughout your day. However, in this chapter, we'll focus on a simple seven-step program that will help you become a more mindful person in your everyday life.

1: Dedicate actual time (and space) for mindfulness practice

It is important for the place you want to practice mindfulness meditation to be quiet and serene. The ideal space has almost nothing in the way of interruption. Sometimes, it is impossible not to have disruptions. However, try and look for the most peaceful space possible. Do not use the space that you set aside for anything else other than meditation and mindfulness. This way, every time you sit down, your body and brain will be notified that it is time to practice meditation.

Here is one way of exercising mindfulness: Sit down with your eyes closed, crisscrossed apple sauce or upright with your back straight. Your hands can rest gently at your side, on your knees or legs. Through this time, it's important to focus on the breath. Let your mind settle, observe your thoughts and visions without judgement or questions. Recognize these thoughts and visions and let them vanish (do not hold on to them), then re-focus on the breath: Inhale…count 1,2,3,4… exhale count 1,2,3,4. This process can be relative to sitting roadside on a bench as a bystander, while watching cars (your thoughts) travel through a busy intersection.

2: Ensure you only focus on the present moment and without judgment

Many people rarely ever consider that the only moment they can live and savor is the present. Do not ponder on the past or the future. Fully accept who you are, at the moment. Someone once said that life is what happens while you are busy making plans for the future, all the while engrossed in your past. Do not allow this to be your definition of life.

3: Allow yourself to just 'be.'

You do not always have to be up and down, trying to fix things and make everything perfect. Your mind and body will be better able to execute tasks if you allow them to recharge.

4: Do not think about the past. Do not plan the future. Do not look at your watch.

It is impossible to change your past. What is done is done. So why waste so much mental energy fussing over things that have happened that are pretty much irreversible? Besides, the future is not here yet. It will come soon enough, but it isn't here yet. Focus on the present moment without saddling yourself with too much worry.

5: Pay close attention to your thoughts, actions, words, and motivations

When you are thinking, what is the reason behind your thoughts? Seek to unearth this reason and give the same treatment to words you say, things you do, Etc. Be deliberate. If you are telling a story to a friend, are you genuinely trying to entertain or benefit them, or are you massaging your ego? You might be surprised at how often your intentions have been self-serving. Always think about motivations behind your thoughts, words, or actions before the fact.

6: Take note of your judgments and let them pass

It is alright to have judgments. Everybody has them. However, you will never truly live a fulfilling, contented life if you live and die by your judgments. Let them be nothing more than fleeting thoughts. Learn to even laugh at them at times. Understand that treating judgments like they are supposed to be permanent is unwise – after all, your mind is susceptible to change.

7: Make sure to return to the present moment

It is alright to be anxious at times. It could be that there are elements in your past that make you queasy. It could be that the future looks uncertain. However, always ensure that you are focused on the 'now.' Understand that you cannot reverse the past or do much to alleviate things coming your way in the future. However, if you are deliberate about your present, it is possible to shape your future the way you want.

The next chapter will answer some frequently asked questions about mindfulness to address any concerns or misconceptions you have about the practice.

Chapter 21: Why You Should Consider Visualizing

Up until now, we've considered using meditation and cognitive restructuring to alter our mental states. But really, it could be the case that visualization is much more beneficial and even more crucial.

The majority of people think that we think in 'thoughts.' That is to say that we come with an internal monologue that operates like the thought boxes in comics. More recent research, however, proposes that we can think in a great deal of techniques:

In some cases we visualize, in some cases, we picture our bodies doing a thing and nearly feeling what we're thinking and occasionally we just 'know.' This latter instance is referred to as 'unsymbolized thought.'

And as a matter of fact, thinking with our bodies and our senses could just be what allowed us to create thought to begin with.

Embodied Cognition

Shortly, embodied cognition is the concept that all our thoughts ultimately connect back to physical experience.

When somebody claims something to you, or when you consider anything, your brain translates this in such a manner that provides it meaning. You don't naturally recognize the language, which indicates the brain must be 'converting' it into some type of pure meaning.

Psychologists at one time believed that the brain had a language of its own that they referred to as 'mentalese.' More recently, though, a growing number of specialists embraced the belief that we comprehend things by visualizing them. When somebody shares with you a story, you comprehend the story since your brain visualizes it occurring to you.

When somebody tells you they went through the snow, you imagine the color white, you picture the cool air on your skin and you nearly hear the noise of the crunching snow underfoot. When we consider 'higher level' thoughts, we comprehend them just because we are able to associate them back to bodily experiences abstraction. Math, besides, is essentially built upon counting.

This is also persistent with the idea that regions of our brain illuminate during visualization as if we were actually engaging in the activity. If you think of swinging a golf club, then neurons associated with that movement will activate in your brain. And as far as your mind and body are involved, that could as well be taking place!

So it makes a bunch of sense to integrate visualization with your meditation practice and with your restructuring. Don't think that visualization can 'trick' your mind into believing something is occurring and thereby change your mood? Then just attempt replaying your most distressing moments, or thinking of scenes from a really sad movie. You'll begin to feel exceptionally sad in a snap.

Visualization for Productivity

One technique to use this power of visualization that is well recognized, is to visit a 'happy place' throughout the meditation. If you can't practice meditation in a quiet and lovely environment, then at the very least you can replicate it in your mind's eye by picturing you're on a stunning beach, in a cabin in the mountains, or in a sizable field receiving plenty of sun. But you can likewise use visualization so as to change your mood in other ways.

For instance, if you're having a hard time concentrating on your work, then you might use visualization to produce a little eustress to inspire you. To accomplish this, you just need to recall why you're performing the work and why it's significant to you.

Let's suggest that you're working towards a demonstration for a meeting. Visualize just how fantastic it would feel to dominate that demonstration and knock it out the park. Then visualize how doing that continuously could someday result in a better career and a better salary, for example. Now visualize the reverse: picture it going wrong and recall why it matters.

You may do the same thing with nearly anything you're having a hard time to focusing on. By connecting what you're doing back to the psychological hook and the main reason you're making it happen, you can a lot more successfully find the dedication and drive you require to accomplish it. Maintain your goals in mind, and you'll be inspired every day to wake up and start exercising, or to focus on your private project, or to put in your greatest performance at work.

Chapter 22: A Simple Explanation Of Mindfulness

Have you ever caught yourself looking out of the window of a train and seeing things in the distance as the train moves forward? The chances are that you have and you give very little credence to the things that you see. There will be towns, villages, scenery and all kinds of other things that you see when you are looking out of that window and the reason you give them very little thought is because they don't affect your life. These are small things that are simply there. When you practice mindfulness, you use a very similar type of thought process. The things are there, happening all around you, but as they do not affect your life, you learn to put no judgment on them. You start to use the senses that you were born with to enjoy what is around you and the most valuable lesson of all when you practice mindfulness is this ability to switch of personal opinion. Life is. It's as simple as that. If you waste your life in retrospective thought, life goes by and the thoughts that you have don't add to what's happening in your life in this moment. If you spend all of your time worrying about what's going to happen tomorrow, it's very similar. It makes little difference to the way that you live your life in this moment. In fact, if anything, it takes away from the enjoyment of the moment.

We are all stressed to the hilt because we measure our own successes in life by what we see all around us. We are not as pretty as some people are. We may not measure up when it comes to the way that we look. The problem is that the consumer world in which we live has presented us with something we don't actually need – information overload – and because of this, we see ourselves as being either superior to or inferior to others. Mindfulness takes you away from all of that. While you still have the knowledge that life has given you, you are taught to enjoy your senses in the now, rather than dwell on thoughts that come from the past or worries from the future, but it doesn't stop there. It is important to learn not to judge. When you judge someone else, you measure yourself and there's absolutely no need to measure yourself. You are unique. You are not something that can be measured.

Mindfulness comes from the Path that was thought up by a Prince centuries before Christ was born. Let me tell you the story so that you understand a little more about what the Buddhist philosophy is all about. This Prince, called Siddhartha Gautama lived in the palace of his father and the life that he lived was fairly well protected. In fact, when he ventured out into the world, he was shocked at the amount of suffering that people had to deal with since he had never experienced this himself. He therefore wanted to know what made people suffer and how they could diminish this suffering and it all came to him after he had meditated and reached the stage which we call "enlightenment." The rules that he devised for living with as little pain as possible are what the Buddhist philosophy is based upon. This involved things such as your approach to life, the amount of effort you put in, the right way to look at things and many different things that still relate to life today. These are not things that are merely confined to Buddhists. Contrary to what many may think Buddhism isn't a religion. It's a philosophy based upon the findings of Siddhartha Gautama and if you apply the mindfulness suggested by him to your life, you will find that you suffer less. I believe, for modern times, something that was said by the current Dalai Lama may hit home. He was asked what surprised him the most about humanity.

""Man. Because he sacrifices his health in order to make money. Then he sacrifices money to recuperate his health. And then he is so anxious about the future that he does not enjoy the present; the result being that he does not live in the present or the future; he lives as if he is never going to die, and then dies having never really lived."

It's a very astute observation of mankind, isn't it? And yet, each of us is guilty of worry about the future or anxious about things that have happened in the past. That's where mindfulness steps in. Mindfulness can be described as being the ability to be perpetually present. That's not a lot to expect of ourselves, but in fact, we are rarely in the present. Sit still for a moment and wipe your mind of thoughts and see how long you last without thoughts creeping into your mind that have no bearing on today. It won't be long because we have been taught that being mindful means thinking about things but it's much more than that.

The other thing that you may not be aware of is that if you incorporate mindfulness into your day, regardless of the duration of your practice, it gets to become a habit and that's when you really benefit from it and start to see the world in a different way. You begin to notice things with all of your senses, instead of being too busy to notice. You also get to feel more inner understanding when you accept that everything is temporary and what's happening NOW won't be happening in five minutes time.

It's time to enjoy the wealth of what life has to offer you and over the course of the next few chapters, I will be showing you how to use mindfulness to improve all areas of your life including your work, your home life and your spirituality and sense of self. It's not new and it's not original. However, I have tried to explain it in a clear way so that you are able to benefit from it to the maximum.

Chapter 23: What Mindfulness Is And How To Practice It

People are baffled when you mention the word "Mindfulness" because they look at practices such as meditation and question whether you are supposed to let go of thoughts. If this is the case, how can you be mindful? Well, there's a difference between being mindless and being mindful. You are not asked to put thoughts out of your head, but you are asked to channel your thoughts into this very moment in time. There lies the difference. The problem with the kind of lives that we live now is that we spend far too much of our mental energy focused upon what we have done in the past or worrying about what we have to do in the future. I think that the best way of summing this up is to use the quotation of the Dalai Lama when he was asked what surprised him about mankind.

Read it again. What the Dalai Lama said has great significance about the approach that most people take to life. We are so busy living our lives with thoughts of what happened to us yesterday that we don't actually give ourselves much time to think about what's happening in our life in this very moment. Another case scenario is that we may be worried about something that is going to happen and thus waste our time in thinking about the future.

From the moment that you are a small child, you are told to mind your manners. You are criticized if you do things wrong and, over the course of a lifetime, may build up a lot of complexes or even develop a low sense of self-esteem based on what other people have said about us or have reacted toward us. With the divorce level being at 50 percent in the

United States, you also have another element that comes into play. People who feel rejected or who feel betrayed often carry those feelings around with them for years and relive the moments of their unsuccessful relationship in the hope that something will change their approach to life or that they avoid making the same mistakes again. The problem with all of this emotional baggage is that it is stopping you from enjoying this very moment in your life.

What I need you to understand is that mindfulness means being in the moment and using all of your senses to enjoy that moment and to be present in it. Just for the sake of argument, let's try an experiment. Put this book down for a moment and observe what is going on around you at this very moment in time. Use your senses. What's the aroma? What sounds are there? What colors are there? What tastes are there?

When you practice mindfulness, you know the answers to these questions. You savor each moment of your life and you are able to observe life in this moment without placing any judgment on it. That's the hard part. In society today, we are taught to judge things to such an extent that people have very negative labels. Fat, skinny, unruly, ugly – these are all descriptions but they are descriptions that have biases that are negative. Our societies have programmed us to see things in either a black or white spectrum. They are either good things or they are bad things. The fact is that mindfulness makes life easier because it places absolutely no judgment on anything. It simply observes.

How it is practiced?

There are several ways of practicing this which I will detail later in the book, but observation, meditation, body scanning and silence are all ways in which we can exercise and practice mindfulness. It helps you in all situations in your life. It improves your blood pressure and heart rate. It helps you to modify your approach to life, helping with stress levels and anger management. The practice of being in the moment can take many forms, but as long as your mind is present and is not distracted into thinking of another time, you are exercising mindfulness to a certain degree. All that you need now is to understand the discipline behind the act of mindfulness.

Chapter 24: Mindfulness Unraveled

To pay attention in a certain way, on purpose, being in the present and not being judgmental. That's how Jon Kabat-Zinn, American professor emeritus of medicine and renowned expert on the subject of mindfulness succinctly described what mindfulness is. Kabat-Zinn also happens to be the creator of the **Stress Reduction Clinic**, and the **Center for Mindfulness in Medicine, Health Care, and Society.**

This is probably one of the best ways to explain what mindfulness really is. To be focused, intentional, being consciously aware of what is happening in the present moment.

Is There Another Way to Describe Mindfulness?

There's a lot of ways you could describe how you understand mindfulness. Everyone is unique and would have their understanding and ways of viewing this practice. At its core, mindfulness is essentially your ability to remain **fully present without being overwhelmed or too reactive to what's going on around you.**

Each one of us is capable of mindfulness. It is a natural ability we possess, and one of the most overlooked tools we have readily available to help us cope with the everyday stressors we encounter with our daily routine. It calls on us to bring our attention and awareness to what we are directly experiencing **at this moment**. Not what happened 5-minutes ago, and not what's going to happen 5-minutes from now. **Focus on what's happening right now.** That's mindfulness, and we need to tap into our senses, thoughts, and current emotions, training our minds to pay attention to our surroundings.

The Mindful Connection Between Your Mind and Body

Mindfulness has been practiced by Buddhist monks for over 2,500 years. Kabat-Zinn only began popularizing this concept in the United States sometime in the late 1970s. He began treating his patients through his **Mindfulness-Based Stress Reduction** technique and experienced great success from those encounters. Since then, numerous studies have been conducted about mindfulness and its mind-body connection. For example, one report which analyzed data from 3,000 participants in 47 clinical trials suggested that because of mindfulness, there were measurable improvements in those experiencing depression and anxiety. An improvement of as much as 20% in fact.

To enhance both your physical and psychological well-being, you're going to have to rely on mindfulness. It is the very element that plays a significant role in helping you learn how to identify and recognize the habitual thought patterns and current behavior patterns you possess which are ingrained in you. Are there certain thought patterns and behaviors that need to be changed? Perhaps, and mindfulness is the only way to discover whether there's a problem that needs to be fixed.

How Mindfulness Can Help You

Admittedly, this is not going to be an easy thing to do. It's not going to be easy having to see clearly for the first time any behavioral or thought patterns that might paint a less than pleasant picture of how you want to see yourself. Chögyam Trungpa, a Tibetan meditation master, once likened this process as if you were to undergo brain surgery without any anesthesia. Or having to listen as insults are being hurled at you one after another. Being a silent observer is not always an easy thing to do, but it is the very reason **why** you need mindfulness to guide you through the process. To learn how to handle and acknowledge these difficult emotions, thoughts, and feelings as you eventually come to a point where you're able to accept what is, and be at peace with it.

Thich Nhat Hanh, a Vietnamese Buddhist monk, and peace activist believes that **"Every mindful step that is taken, every mindful breath that is made, is establishing peace in the present and**

preventing war in the future. When you transform your consciousness, the process begins to change the collective consciousness." Wise words indeed, because if you're not first at peace with yourself, you can never find peace with the rest of the world. To become present, you must first **realize that you're not present**. Like waking up from a nap, and opening your eyes to clearly see what's in front of you.

Whenever we choose to do something, it's usually because there is some benefit to be gained. Mindfulness is no different. In fact, you've probably decided to give this a try **because** you're hoping it can alleviate that heavy, stressful burden you've been carrying around with you for far too long. You're looking for a release, something to take the nervous edge, anxiety, and "the weight of the world on your shoulders" feeling. A way to minimize the emotional outbursts that happen because of stress, mood swings, tendency to overthink, and to return the happiness that seems to have eluded you for long enough as stress took its place.

That's how you arrived at mindfulness, and the good news is, you've come to the right place. Mindfulness is going to help you:

• **Improve Your Health (Physically)** - Taking care of your mental health is going to go a long way towards how you feel physically. Scientists have made an interesting discovery about how mindfulness is the key to reclaiming physical health and vitality. By minimizing the symptoms of stress that are experienced, it effectively lowers all the other symptoms that could manifest as a product of stress. Lower blood pressure, less chronic muscular aches and pains, better sleep, better gastrointestinal functioning, and minimizing the risk of heart disease are some of the many benefits that await you with regular mindful practice.

- **Regain Your Well-Being** - It is difficult to live a happy, healthy, and satisfying life when stress gets in the way. Practicing mindfulness is a way to reclaim that lost well-being as you learn to cherish and appreciate the little things in life once again by focusing on your present. It's easy to feel like life is terrible, or wonder why bad things always happen to you when you let the negativity of stress get in the way. You lose sight of the present when you don't stop to think about what's happening around you. It is through mindfulness that you are going to focus on being less preoccupied with what you **cannot control**, and focus instead on appreciating what you are going through right now.

- **Stop Speculating** - To live calmly in the present, you need to learn to see things as they are. The mind can easily get carried away and run wild if we allow it to, which is how we end up worrying more than we should be over things that we sometimes may not be able to control. The goal of mindfulness is to be able to acknowledge what you are going through. To acknowledge that y**es, this is happening to you right now**, and I can accept it. To train yourself to observe the present moment and accept it for what it is.

• **Be Kind** - We're quick to show kindness to others, but hesitate when it comes to ourselves. We're guilty of being too hard on ourselves, which only adds to the stress that we already feel on top of everything else. You beat yourself up more than you should, and it only through mindfulness that you can finally break free of this habit. How? By reminding you to bring yourself back to the present again, and again, each time that your mind has wandered off more than it should towards negative, worrying, and obsessive thoughts. When you do catch your thoughts wandering, pay attention to it, put a stop to it, and switch your train of thought. Use mindfulness to bring yourself back to your present.

Conclusion

Thank you for making it through to the end of this book, let's hope it was informative and able to provide you with all of the tools you need to achieve your goals whatever they may be.

Stress is a real issue, and it affects all of us on some level. The problem is that most of us are never able to identify its real extent before it is too late.

Even simple behavioral changes can reflect stress in life, but most of us remain ignorant about them.

Stress not only affects us emotionally and behaviorally, but it also has a deep and severe physiological impact on which most people remain completely unaware.

Not knowing something doesn't mean it would affect us any less.

If stress is not encountered at the right time, getting over it can be very difficult.

Many people keep struggling all their lives but are never fully able to recover.

Most people completely surrender to unchangeable stressors and are forced to spend miserable lives, although they had a real chance to recover.

This book has tried to cover all that so that you don't remain affected due to ignorance and get a real chance to overcome stress in life.

This book has laid out plans, tips and tricks, and practical techniques through which you can overcome stress.

I hope that you will be able to make use of this information in a practical and meaningful way.

Every effort has been made to ensure the accuracy of the facts.

I hope that you will be able to reap the benefits of mindfulness in your personal life, and this book would be useful in the process.

www.ingramcontent.com/pod-product-compliance
Lightning Source LLC
Chambersburg PA
CBHW072014070526
44583CB00015B/1480